Gooseberry Patch

Everyday Simple Suppers

Everyday Simple Suppers

©2013 by Gooseberry Patch
2500 Farmers Dr., #110, Columbus, Ohio 43235
1-800-854-6673, **gooseberrypatch.com**

©2013 by Time Home Entertainment Inc.
135 West 50th Street, New York, NY 10020

ISBN-13: 978-0-8487-3982-9   ISBN-10: 0-8487-3982-5

Library of Congress Control Number: 2012949214
Printed in the United States of America
First Printing 2013

Oxmoor House
Editorial Director: Leah McLaughlin
Creative Director: Felicity Keane
Brand Manager: Vanessa Tiongson
Senior Editor: Rebecca Brennan
Managing Editor: Rebecca Benton

Gooseberry Patch Everyday Simple Suppers
Editor: Ashley T. Strickland
Art Director: Claire Cormany
Assistant Designer: Allison Sperando Potter
Director, Test Kitchen: Elizabeth Tyler Austin
Assistant Directors, Test Kitchen: Julie Christopher, Julie Gunter
Recipe Developers and Testers: Wendy Ball, R.D.; Victoria E. Cox;
    Tamara Goldis; Stefanie Maloney; Callie Nash; Karen Rankin;
    Leah Van Deren
Recipe Editor: Alyson Moreland Haynes
Food Stylists: Margaret Monroe Dickey, Catherine Crowell Steele
Photography Director: Jim Bathie
Senior Photographer: Hélène Dujardin
Senior Photo Stylist: Kay E. Clarke
Photo Stylist: Mindi Shapiro Levine
Assistant Photo Stylist: Mary Louise Menendez
Senior Production Manager: Greg A. Amason

Contributors
Project Editor: Katie Strasser
Recipe Developers and Testers: Erica Hopper, Tonya Johnson,
    Kyra Moncrief, Kathleen Royal Phillips
Copy Editors: Norma Butterworth-McKittrick, Rhonda Lother
Proofreader: Rhonda Lother
Interns: Megan Branagh, Frances Gunnells, Susan Kemp, Sara Lyon,
    Staley McIlwain, Jeffrey Preis, Maria Sanders, Julia Sayers
Food Stylist: Libbie Summers
Photographer: Mary Britton Senseney
Photo Stylists: Elizabeth Demos

Time Home Entertainment Inc.
Publisher: Jim Childs
VP, Strategy & Business Development: Steven Sandonato
Executive Director, Marketing Services: Carol Pittard
Executive Director, Retail & Special Sales: Tom Mifsud
Director, Bookazine Development & Marketing: Laura Adam
Executive Publishing Director: Joy Butts
Associate Publishing Director: Megan Pearlman
Finance Director: Glenn Buonocore
Associate General Counsel: Helen Wan

To order additional publications, call 1-800-765-6400 or 1-800-491-0551.

For more books to enrich your life, visit **oxmoorhouse.com**
To search, savor, and share thousands of recipes, visit **myrecipes.com**

Front Cover (from left to right, top to bottom): Brenda's Fruit Crisp *(page 249)*, Chicken Cordon Bleu *(page 8)*, Pepper Steak *(page 48)*

Page 1: Barbecue Chicken Kabobs *(page 43)*

Back Cover (from left to right, top to bottom): Slow-Cooker Beefy Taco Soup *(page 31)*, Veggie Mini Pizzas *(page 116)*

Dear Friend,

After a busy day of work, soccer practices and ballet lessons, nothing quite satisfies your hungry family like a comforting home-cooked meal. But who has the time? With *Gooseberry Patch Everyday Simple Suppers,* you do! Jam-packed with more than 250 down-home delicious recipes that are easy to prepare, this book allows you to have dinner on the table in a snap.

What's not to love about Lemony Pork Piccata (page 90)? It cooks up quick and only uses one dish, so clean-up is done before you can say lickety-split! Serve it with some quick-cooking angel hair pasta and Country-Time Green Beans (page 209), and you've got a complete meal the whole family will love! Pizza is always a hit, so we've included a chapter devoted solely to scrumptious pizza and pasta recipes. Try Mexican Pizza (page 107) or Linda's Spring Greens Pizza (page 114) for an all-in-one dinner. Didn't make it to the grocery store today? Don't worry! You probably already have the ingredients for the family favorite Cheeseburger Bake (page 30) in your pantry, refrigerator and freezer!

Everyday Simple Suppers is your solution to preparing wholesome dinners in a jiffy without sacrificing taste. This brand-new collection of tried & true favorites offers a variety of slow-cooker recipes, 5-ingredient recipes, one-dish recipes and even quick-to-fix desserts such as Gooey Toffee Scotchies (page 226) to indulge your sweet tooth. So bypass the drive-through this evening and serve up something yummy from *Everyday Simple Suppers.* We know you'll love it!

Wishing you delicious dinners,

JoAnn & Vickie

Buffalo Chicken Wing Soup,
page 21

contents

Broccoli-Chicken
Casserole, page 18

one-dish wonders

Making weeknight family meals is easy when you turn to these one-pot winners. From cozy casseroles such as Poppy Seed Chicken (page 13) and Quick & Easy Shepherd's Pie (page 26) to sensational slow-cooker suppers such as Joan's Slow-Cooker Chicken Stuffing Casserole (page 19) and Best-Ever Slow-Cooker Shredded Beef Tacos (page 23), you'll always have an answer for "what's for dinner?"

Chicken Cordon Bleu

5 boneless, skinless chicken
   breasts, pounded thin
salt and pepper to taste
1 T. fresh chives, chopped
10 thin slices cooked ham
10 slices American cheese

10 slices bacon
10¾-oz. can cream of
   mushroom soup
1 c. whipping cream
Garnish: fresh chives, chopped

Sprinkle each chicken breast with salt and pepper to taste; top with chives. Place 2 slices of ham and 2 slices of cheese on each chicken breast; roll up each breast. Wrap 2 slices of bacon around each roll; secure with wooden toothpicks. Place in a lightly greased 13"x9" baking pan; bake, uncovered, at 350 degrees for 45 minutes. Heat mushroom soup and cream in a heavy saucepan over medium heat until smooth and heated through, stirring constantly. To serve, ladle sauce over chicken breasts; garnish with chives. Serves 5.

Glenda Tebbens
Lincoln, DE

Stuffed Artichoke Chicken

"This is one of my husband's favorite meals. The filling was originally served as an appetizer. One day I decided to try filling chicken cutlets with it, and it was a big hit!"
–Michelle

1 c. mayonnaise
1 onion, chopped
1 c. grated Parmesan cheese
14-oz. can artichoke hearts,
   drained and chopped
1 T. lemon juice
½ t. pepper

2 lbs. boneless chicken cutlets
salt and pepper to taste
3 T. olive oil
¾ c. seasoned dry bread
   crumbs
Garnish: fresh sage

Combine mayonnaise, onion, cheese, artichokes, lemon juice and ½ teaspoon pepper in a bowl; set aside. Flatten chicken cutlets between 2 pieces of wax paper until thin; sprinkle with salt and pepper. Spread artichoke mixture onto each chicken cutlet. Roll up; secure with wooden toothpicks. Drizzle roll-ups with oil; coat with bread crumbs. Place in an ungreased 13"x9" baking pan. Bake, uncovered, at 350 degrees for 30 minutes. Garnish with sage. Serves 8.

Michelle Marckesano
East Meadow, NY

Stuffed Artichoke
Chicken

Slow-Cooker Creamy Apricot Chicken
Tami Hoffman (Litchfield, NH)

Serve with velvety mashed potatoes and your favorite veggie. Then pour on spoonfuls of the savory apricot sauce.

8-oz. bottle Russian salad dressing

12-oz. jar apricot preserves

1 to 2 lbs. boneless, skinless chicken breasts

Combine salad dressing and preserves; set aside. Arrange chicken in a 5-quart slow cooker; pour dressing mixture on top. Cover and cook on high setting for one hour and then on low setting for 3 hours, or until chicken juices run clear. Serves 4 to 6.

Sour Cream Chicken Rolls

Impress your guests with this entrée, and they'll keep coming back for more! It is simple, yummy and makes a nice presentation.

4 boneless, skinless chicken breasts
16-oz. container sour cream
6-oz. pkg. stuffing mix, crushed
6.2-oz. pkg. long-grain and wild rice mix, cooked

Place chicken breasts between 2 pieces of plastic wrap; pound to flatten slightly. Brush sour cream over chicken, coating both sides well. Dip into stuffing mix, coating both sides. Discard any remaining stuffing mix. Roll up chicken; secure with wooden toothpicks. Place in a lightly greased 9"x9" baking pan; cover with aluminum foil. Bake at 350 degrees for 30 minutes. Remove foil; bake for another 15 minutes, or until chicken juices run clear. Slice roll-ups into spirals. Serve over cooked rice. Serves 4.

Joanne Wilson
Roselle Park, NJ

"My friend shared this recipe with me many years ago. I still request it whenever she asks me over for dinner. The leftover chicken even makes a delicious cold sandwich the next day...give it a try!"

—Joanne

Poppy Seed
Chicken

Baked Potatoes + Chicken Sauce

A few simple ingredients turn baked potatoes into a filling, comforting meal.

4 baking potatoes
1 to 2 t. oil
2 5-oz. cans chicken, drained and flaked
1 c. sour cream
½ c. mayonnaise
4 t. milk
½ t. seasoned salt
¼ t. pepper
Optional: fresh parsley, chopped

Pierce skins of potatoes several times with a fork; rub oil lightly over potatoes. Bake at 350 degrees for about one hour, until tender. Combine chicken, sour cream, mayonnaise, milk, seasoned salt and pepper in a small saucepan over low heat. Heat until hot and bubbly, stirring occasionally. Slice baked potatoes in half lengthwise; place each potato on a plate. Spoon chicken mixture over potatoes. Sprinkle with parsley, if desired. Serves 4.

Karie Rittenour
Columbus, OH

Poppy Seed Chicken

2 lbs. boneless, skinless chicken breasts, cooked and cubed
10¾-oz. can cream of chicken soup
1 c. sour cream
½ c. butter or margarine, melted
2 T. poppy seed
1 sleeve round buttery crackers, crushed and divided
Garnish: chopped fresh parsley

Combine all ingredients except cracker crumbs and garnish; spread in an ungreased 13"x9" baking pan. Sprinkle with cracker crumbs; bake, uncovered, at 350 degrees for 30 minutes, or until chicken juices run clear. Garnish with parsley. Serves 6.

Julie Diedrich
McPherson, KS

supper in a snap

Casseroles can often be made ahead and refrigerated. Just be sure to let them stand at room temperature for 30 minutes before baking.

Crispy Pecan-Chicken Casserole

Michelle Greeley (Hayes, VA)

2 c. cooked chicken, chopped
½ c. chopped pecans
2 T. onion, finely chopped
¾ c. celery, sliced
1 c. mayonnaise
½ c. sour cream

10¾-oz. can cream of chicken
  soup
2 t. lemon juice
1 c. potato chips, crushed
1 c. shredded Cheddar cheese

Mix together all ingredients except chips and cheese. Place in a lightly greased 3-quart casserole dish. Combine chips and cheese; sprinkle on top. Bake, uncovered, at 375 degrees for 30 to 35 minutes, until golden and bubbly. Serves 6.

Chicken Marimba

Everyone loves this cheesy casserole…it's a potluck favorite!

½ c. onion, chopped
½ c. green pepper, chopped
1 c. sliced mushrooms
2 T. butter
10¾-oz. can cream of chicken soup
⅓ c. milk
¼ c. pimento, chopped
½ t. dried basil

4 oz. bowtie pasta, cooked and drained
1½ c. cottage cheese
3 c. cooked chicken, diced
2 c. shredded Cheddar cheese
½ c. fresh Parmesan cheese, grated
Garnish: fresh cilantro, chopped

Sauté onion, pepper and mushrooms in butter in a skillet over medium heat until tender; stir in soup, milk, pimento and basil. Layer half the pasta and half the soup mixture in bottom of a 13"x9" baking pan. Stir cottage cheese until smooth; spread half over pasta and soup. Add layers of half the cooked chicken, half the Cheddar cheese and half the Parmesan cheese. Repeat layers. Bake at 350 degrees for 45 minutes to one hour. Garnish with cilantro. Serves 6 to 8.

Kristine Marumoto
Sandy, UT

perfect pasta

So many favorite comfort food recipes begin with pasta or noodles. The secret to perfectly cooked pasta is to use plenty of cooking water…about a gallon per pound of pasta in a very large pot.

Pat's Chicken + Wild Rice Casserole

This is such an elegant casserole, and it's a great way to use leftover chicken. You can also assemble it the night before and bake it the next day.

toss-ins for a twist

Change the flavor of this casserole by adding slivered almonds, chopped red cherry peppers or minced garlic. Try chopped, cooked turkey breast too.

2 6.2-oz. pkgs. long-grain and wild rice mix
4½ c. chicken broth
¼ c. butter, divided
3 to 4 celery stalks, chopped
1 onion, chopped
6 to 8 boneless, skinless chicken breasts, cooked and cubed

2 10¾-oz. cans cream of chicken soup
8-oz. container sour cream
Optional: crushed potato chips
Garnish: chopped fresh parsley

Prepare rice according to package directions, using broth instead of water and 2 tablespoons butter. Sauté celery and onion in remaining butter in a skillet over medium heat until crisp-tender. Combine rice with chicken, celery mixture, soup and sour cream in a large bowl. Spoon into a greased 13"x9" baking pan. Top with crushed potato chips, if desired. Bake, uncovered, at 350 degrees for 30 minutes, or until hot and bubbly. Garnish with parsley. Serves 8 to 10.

Pat Beach
Fisherville, KY

wrap it up

If you're taking a casserole along to a potluck or carry-in, secure the lid with a brightly colored tea towel wrapped around the baking dish and knotted at the top. Keep the serving spoon handy by tucking it through the knot.

Broccoli-Chicken Casserole

This hearty one-dish dinner goes together oh-so quickly! It's a tasty way to turn leftover chicken into a second meal.

supper in a snap

Rotisserie chicken from the deli is such a great convenience item. Use it here instead of cooking chicken to save time.

10¾-oz. can cream of mushroom soup
1½ c. milk
6-oz. pkg. chicken-flavored stuffing mix
3 c. cooked chicken, cubed

10-oz. pkg. frozen chopped broccoli, thawed
1 onion, finely chopped
2 stalks celery, finely chopped
Optional: ½ c. shredded mozzarella cheese

Whisk together soup and milk in a large bowl. Stir in remaining ingredients except cheese; mix well. Spoon into a lightly greased 3-quart casserole dish. Bake, uncovered, at 350 degrees for 35 to 40 minutes. Sprinkle with cheese during the last 10 minutes of baking time, if desired. Serves 4 to 6.

Gladys Brehm
Quakertown, PA

Joan's Slow-Cooker Chicken Stuffing Casserole

Hearty and filling, this chicken dish will be the first to disappear at any potluck.

2 6-oz. pkgs. chicken-flavored
  stuffing mix
2 10¾-oz. cans cream of
  chicken soup, divided

½ c. milk
3 c. cooked chicken, cubed
8-oz. pkg. shredded Cheddar
  cheese

Prepare stuffing mix according to package directions; place in a lightly greased 5-quart slow cooker. Stir in one can soup. Stir together remaining soup, milk and chicken in a separate bowl. Add to slow cooker. Sprinkle cheese over top. Cover and cook on high setting for 3 hours or on low setting for 4 to 6 hours. Serves 6.

Joan Brochu
Harwich, MA

Chicken Fajita Chowder

This chunky chowder is full of Mexican flavor! Serve it with a variety of tortilla chips for an added burst of color.

3 T. all-purpose flour
1.4-oz. pkg. fajita or taco seasoning mix, divided
4 boneless, skinless chicken breasts, cubed
3 T. vegetable oil
1 onion, chopped
1 t. garlic, minced
15¼-oz. can sweet corn and diced peppers, drained
15-oz. can black beans, drained and rinsed
14½-oz. can Mexican-style stewed tomatoes

4.5-oz. can chopped green chiles
3 c. water
1 c. instant brown rice, uncooked
10¾-oz. can nacho cheese soup
1¼ c. water
Toppings: sour cream, shredded Cheddar cheese, chopped green onions, tortilla chips
Garnish: fresh cilantro sprigs

Combine flour and 2 tablespoons seasoning mix in a large plastic zipping bag; add chicken. Seal bag and shake to coat. Sauté chicken in hot oil in a large Dutch oven over high heat about 5 minutes, until golden, stirring often. Reduce heat to medium-high. Add onion and garlic; sauté 5 minutes. Stir in remaining seasoning mix, corn, beans, tomatoes, chiles, 3 cups water and rice; bring to a boil. Reduce heat to medium-low; cover and simmer 5 minutes. Add soup and 1¼ cups water; stir until thoroughly heated. Sprinkle with desired toppings; garnish with fresh cilantro. Serves 8 to 10.

Kelly Jones
Tallahassee, FL

supper in a snap

This chowder serves a crowd, which means you'll most likely have leftovers. Freeze any remaining soup, without the toppings, for busy days...you'll be glad you did!

Buffalo Chicken Wing Soup

Anna McMaster (Portland, OR)

Keep hot sauce on the table for those who would like an extra dash.

6 c. milk
3 10¾-oz. cans cream of chicken
   soup
3 c. chicken, cooked and shredded

1 c. sour cream
¼ to ½ c. hot pepper sauce
Garnish: shredded Monterey Jack
cheese, chopped green onions

Combine all ingredients except garnish in a 5-quart slow cooker. Cover and cook on low setting for 4 to 5 hours. To serve, garnish with cheese and onions. Serves 8.

Homemade Turkey Pot Pie

This recipe has been in our family for years...a real treat.

⅓ c. butter
⅓ c. onion, chopped
⅓ c. all-purpose flour
½ t. salt
¼ t. pepper
1¾ c. turkey broth
⅔ c. milk

2½ to 3 c. cooked turkey, chopped
10-oz. pkg. frozen peas and carrots, thawed
14.1-oz pkg. refrigerated pie crusts

Melt butter in a large saucepan over low heat. Stir in onion, flour, salt and pepper. Cook, stirring constantly, until mixture is bubbly; remove from heat. Stir in broth and milk. Heat to boiling, stirring constantly. Boil and stir for one minute. Mix in turkey and peas and carrots; set aside. Roll out one pie crust and place in a 9"x9" baking pan. Pour turkey mixture into pan. Roll remaining crust into an 11-inch square; cut out vents with a small cookie cutter. Place crust over filling; turn edges under and crimp. Bake at 425 degrees for 35 minutes, or until golden. Serves 4 to 6.

Sarah Sullivan
Andrews, NC

pick the right size

Choosing a turkey? Allow about one pound per person plus a little extra for leftovers. For example, a 15-pound turkey would serve 12 people with enough left to enjoy this turkey pot pie, turkey sandwiches, turkey tetrazzini or turkey soup afterward.

Best-Ever Slow-Cooker Shredded Beef Tacos

Two for one! The first night, I make tacos with this recipe. The second night, I add barbecue sauce to the remaining beef and make barbecue beef sandwiches.

3 to 5-lb. beef chuck roast
1 c. water
½ red onion, chopped
3 cloves garlic, chopped
1 T. cayenne pepper
2 t. ground cumin
2 t. dried oregano
1 t. pepper
¼ c. oil
taco shells
Garnish: favorite toppings such as shredded lettuce, chopped tomatoes, shredded cheese, sour cream and guacamole

toss-ins for a twist

This recipe is delicious with boneless pork or chicken, too! They also make great barbecue sandwiches.

Place roast in a slow cooker; add water and set aside. Combine onion, garlic, spices and oil in a blender. Process until well mixed and pour over roast. Cover and cook on high setting for 6 to 7 hours, until roast is tender. Break roast apart with a fork. Reduce setting to low; cover and cook one more hour. To serve, spoon into taco shells; garnish as desired. Serves 6 to 10.

Kathy Lowe
Orem, UT

Easy Slow-Cooker Sauerbraten Beef

"This recipe is simply wonderful. There's a delicious aroma when you walk into the house...and what a nice, comforting meal to have after a long day at work."

—Denise

16 gingersnap cookies
2 lbs. London broil beef steak, sliced into ½-inch thick strips
10¾-oz. can French onion soup
⅔ c. water
½ c. white vinegar
¼ c. oil
potato pancakes or cooked egg noodles
Garnish: fresh parsley, chopped

Place cookies into a gallon-size plastic zipping bag and crush. Add beef strips to bag; close bag and shake thoroughly until coated. Transfer entire contents of bag to a slow cooker. Combine soup, water, vinegar and oil in a bowl; pour over beef mixture. Cover and cook on low setting for 6 to 8 hours. Serve over potato pancakes or cooked noodles. Garnish with parsley. Serves 4 to 6.

Denise Frederick
Climax, NY

Mama's Meatloaf
Maxine Blakely (Seneca, SC)

1½ lbs. ground beef
2 eggs, beaten
¾ c. milk
⅔ c. saltine cracker crumbs
salt and pepper to taste

Optional: 2 t. onion, chopped
¼ c. catsup
2 t. brown sugar, packed
1 t. mustard
1 T. lemon juice

Mix together beef, eggs, milk, cracker crumbs, salt, pepper and onion, if desired, in a large bowl. Form into a loaf and place in an ungreased 9"x5" loaf pan. Bake, covered, at 350 degrees for 45 minutes. Mix remaining ingredients; spread over meatloaf. Bake, uncovered, 15 more minutes. Serves 6 to 8.

Quick + Easy Shepherd's Pie

This low-fuss meal makes delicious leftovers…if you have any!

1¼ lbs. ground beef
1 onion, chopped
8-oz. can tomato sauce
8-oz. can green beans, drained
8-oz. can corn, drained
¼ t. cumin
½ t. garlic powder
¼ t. salt
1 lb. pkg. refrigerated mashed
  potatoes
1 egg, beaten
2½ c. shredded Monterey Jack
  cheese, divided
Garnish: fresh parsley, chopped

Brown beef with onion; drain. Stir in tomato sauce, green beans, corn, cumin, garlic powder and salt; simmer while preparing mashed potatoes according to package directions. Combine egg and 2 cups cheese in a separate mixing bowl; spread in the bottom of a lightly greased 8"x8" baking pan. Spoon meat mixture over cheese; spread potatoes on top. Sprinkle with remaining cheese; bake, uncovered, at 375 degrees for 20 to 30 minutes. Let stand 5 minutes before serving. Garnish with parsley. Serves 9.

Toni Wilcox
Winter Park, FL

family message board

Hang an old-fashioned washboard for a whimsical way to keep notes organized. Hot-glue magnets to old-fashioned wooden clip clothespins to hold notes and photos in place.

Cornbread-Topped BBQ Beef

2 lbs. ground beef
1 onion, diced
1 green pepper, diced
11-oz. can corn, drained

14½-oz. can diced tomatoes,
  drained
½ c. barbecue sauce
3 8½-oz. pkgs. cornbread mix

Brown beef and onion in a skillet over medium heat; drain. Add vegetables; cook and stir until tender. Stir in sauce; spread mixture in an ungreased 13"x9" baking pan. Prepare cornbread mix according to package directions; spread batter over beef mixture. Bake, uncovered, at 400 degrees for 20 to 25 minutes, until golden and a knife tip inserted in center comes out clean. Serves 8 to 10.

Megan Brooks
Antioch, TN

"My sister shared this recipe with me, and it has quickly become a family favorite. Not only is it super-easy to make, but it's also a good chance for me to sneak in some veggies for my picky eaters!"
—Megan

Sour Cream-Beef Casserole

This recipe was passed to me many years ago…it's a family favorite.

12-oz. pkg. wide egg noodles
1 lb. ground beef
29-oz. can tomato sauce
½ t. salt
⅛ t. pepper
⅛ t. dried oregano
1 c. sour cream

⅔ c. cream cheese, softened
½ onion, finely chopped
½ green pepper, minced
2 c. shredded mozzarella
  cheese, divided
Garnish: fresh parsley

Prepare noodles according to package directions; drain and set aside. Meanwhile, brown beef in a skillet over medium heat; drain. Stir in tomato sauce and seasonings. Combine noodles with sour cream, cream cheese, onion and green pepper; mix well. Spread half the noodle mixture in an ungreased 13"x9" baking pan. Layer half the beef mixture over top; sprinkle with half the mozzarella cheese. Repeat layers. Bake, uncovered, at 350 degrees for 20 to 25 minutes, until hot and bubbly. Garnish with parsley. Serves 12.

Mary Burns
Hurricane, WV

Nacho Grande Casserole

Turn this chunky casserole into a hearty appetizer by providing tortilla chips for dipping.

2 lbs. ground beef
1 onion, chopped
2 16-oz. cans spicy chili beans
16-oz. pkg. frozen corn, thawed
15-oz. can tomato sauce
1¼-oz. pkg. taco seasoning mix

3 c. finely shredded Cheddar
   Jack cheese, divided
3 c. nacho cheese tortilla
   chips, crushed and divided
Toppings: chopped tomatoes,
   green onions

Cook beef and onion in a Dutch oven over medium-high heat, stirring until beef crumbles and is no longer pink; drain. Add beans, corn, tomato sauce and seasoning mix; stir until blended. Simmer over medium heat 10 minutes. Pour half of beef mixture into a lightly greased 13"x9" baking pan. Top with 1½ cups each of cheese and crushed chips; top with remaining beef mixture and remaining 1½ cups each of cheese and chips. Bake at 350 degrees for 25 to 30 minutes, until bubbly and golden. Sprinkle with chopped tomatoes and green onions, if desired. Serves 8 to 10.

Carol Hickman
Kingsport, TN

busy day hint

If family members will be eating at different times, spoon casserole ingredients into individual ramekins for baking. Each person can enjoy their own fresh-from-the-oven mini casserole.

Cheeseburger Bake

For a neighbor in need or a new mom, duplicate this recipe using a 9" round disposable aluminum foil pan.

8-oz. tube refrigerated crescent rolls
1 lb. ground beef, browned
1¼-oz. pkg. taco seasoning mix
15-oz. can tomato sauce
2 c. shredded Cheddar cheese

Unroll crescent roll dough; press into a greased 9" round baking pan, pinching seams closed. Bake, uncovered, at 350 degrees for 10 minutes; set aside. Combine beef, seasoning mix and tomato sauce in a 12" skillet; heat through, about 7 minutes. Pour into crust; sprinkle cheese on top. Bake, uncovered, for 10 to 15 minutes. Let stand 5 minutes before serving. Serves 4.

Jennifer Dutcher
Lewis Center, OH

Potato Puff Casserole

My family loves this dish served with green beans and dinner rolls. It's so simple that I'm always happy to fix it for them!

2 lbs. ground beef
10¾-oz. can cream of mushroom soup
10¾-oz. can cream of chicken soup
1⅓ c. milk
6 c. frozen potato puffs
1½ c. shredded Cheddar cheese

Brown beef in a skillet over medium heat; drain. Stir in soups and milk; heat through. Spoon into an ungreased 13"x9" baking pan. Layer potato puffs evenly over top. Bake, uncovered, at 375 degrees for 25 minutes, or until puffs are golden. Sprinkle with cheese. Bake an additional 5 minutes, or until cheese melts. Serves 8 to 10.

Tina George
El Dorado, AR

Slow-Cooker Beefy Taco Soup

Erin McRae (Beaverton, OR)

Top each bowl of this hearty soup with sour cream and a sprinkling of shredded cheese.

1 lb. ground beef, browned
14½-oz. can stewed tomatoes
15-oz. can kidney beans, drained
   and rinsed
1¼-oz. env. taco seasoning mix
8-oz. can tomato sauce

Stir together all ingredients; pour into a 3- to 4-quart slow cooker. Cover and cook on low setting for 6 to 8 hours; stir occasionally. Serves 4 to 6.

Slow-Cooker Sauerkraut Pork Roast

Just add mashed potatoes...everyone will beg for seconds!

3 to 4-lb. **pork roast**
1 T. **oil**

salt and **pepper** to taste
15-oz. can **sauerkraut**

Brown pork roast on all sides in oil in a skillet over high heat. Sprinkle with salt and pepper. Place roast in a 5-quart slow cooker; top with sauerkraut. Cover and cook on low setting for 6 to 8 hours. Serves 6 to 8.

Teresa McBee
Billings, MT

Purlieu

Pronounced PEARL-yew, and also called Chicken Bog, this is a South Carolina Low Country recipe. Always a favorite dish found at church socials, family reunions, potlucks and family dinners.

14-oz. pkg. smoked sausage, sliced ¼-inch thick
4 slices bacon, chopped
1 onion, chopped
4 c. chicken broth
4 boneless, skinless chicken breasts, cut into bite-size pieces
5-oz. saffron yellow rice, uncooked
1¼ c. long-cooking rice, uncooked
Garnish: fresh parsley

toss-ins for a twist

Stir in cooked shrimp at the end for an extra boost of flavor.

Combine sausage, bacon and onion in a large pot over medium heat. Sauté until onion is translucent. Add broth; bring to a boil. Stir in chicken; return to a boil again. Add yellow and long-cooking rice; boil for one minute. Reduce heat to low; cover and cook for 20 minutes. Remove from heat; let stand covered for 10 minutes. Garnish with parsley. Serves 8.

Cheri Mason
Harmony, NC

Easy Italian Wedding Soup

Though you probably won't see this recipe on the menu at many weddings, it is a traditional Italian soup that's often served for holidays and other special events.

"We sprinkle each serving with freshly shredded Parmesan cheese."

—Debby

2 14½-oz. cans chicken broth
1 c. water
1 c. medium shell pasta, uncooked
16 frozen meatballs, cooked

2 c. spinach leaves, finely shredded
1 cup pizza sauce
Optional: shredded Parmesan cheese

Bring broth and water to a boil in a large saucepan; add pasta and meatballs. Return to a boil; cook 7 to 9 minutes, until pasta is done. Do not drain. Reduce heat; stir in spinach and pizza sauce. Cook one to 2 minutes, until thoroughly heated. Sprinkle with Parmesan cheese, if desired. Serves 4.

Debby Horton
Cincinnati, OH

Hearty Pierogie Casserole

2 to 3 16.9-oz. pkgs. frozen favorite-flavor pierogies
1½ to 2 lbs. smoked pork sausage, sliced into bite-size pieces

26-oz. can cream of mushroom soup
3¼ c. milk
2 to 3 c. shredded Cheddar cheese

Bring a large saucepan of water to a boil; add pierogies and sausage. Cook for 5 to 7 minutes, until pierogies float; drain. Arrange pierogie mixture in a lightly greased 13"x9" baking dish. Blend soup and milk; pour over top of pierogie mixture. Top with cheese. Bake, uncovered, at 350 degrees for 30 to 35 minutes, until soup mixture is bubbly and cheese is lightly golden. Let stand for 5 minutes before serving. Serves 8.

Sheryl Maksymoski
Grand Rapids, MI

Easy Italian
Wedding Soup

Baked Crumbed Haddock

Michelle Waddington (New Bedford, MA)

Delicious! Serve with mac & cheese and steamed broccoli for a down-home dinner.

2 5½-oz. pkgs. onion & garlic
   croutons
1 c. butter, melted

3 lbs. haddock fillets
Optional: lemon slices

Finely grind croutons in a food processor. Toss together croutons and butter. Place fish in a lightly greased 13"x9" baking pan. Sprinkle crouton mixture over fish. Bake, uncovered, at 350 degrees for 20 to 25 minutes, until fish flakes easily with a fork. Top fish with lemon slices, if desired. Serves 6 to 8.

Tomato-Mushroom Grilled Fish

This is a wonderful recipe for the summer months, and baking in parchment paper or aluminum foil packets makes clean-up a breeze. You can use orange roughy, sea bass or halibut.

1 T. butter, softened
4 c. baby spinach
2 6-oz. white fish fillets,
  ½-inch thick
salt and pepper to taste
½ c. zucchini, cut into thin
  slivers

4 mushrooms, sliced
1 tomato, chopped
¼ c. fresh basil, chopped
2 T. lime juice
1 T. olive oil

For each packet, layer 3 sheets of parchment paper or two 15-inch pieces of aluminum foil. Spread butter down center of each piece. Lay 2 cups spinach on buttered area of each paper. Place fish on top; sprinkle with salt and pepper to taste. Divide zucchini, mushrooms and tomato evenly on top of fish. Sprinkle with basil, lime juice and oil. To seal, fold one long edge of paper or foil over the other; tuck short ends underneath. Be certain packets are tightly wrapped so that juices will not escape. Place on a baking sheet. Bake at 450 degrees for 15 to 18 minutes, until fish flakes. When ready to serve, arrange fish and vegetables on plates. Serves 2.

Sharon Demers
Dolores, CO

toss-ins for a twist

Chicken breasts pounded to ½-inch thickness are also great as a substitute for fish.

now & later

Serve Tomato-Mushroom Grilled Fish with boil-in-bag steamed rice. Make some extra and freeze one-cup portions in plastic zipping bags. You'll have a quick side on hand for extra-busy nights.

Spiced-Up Tuna-Noodle Casserole

Mom always made tuna noodle casserole, and this is her recipe...but updated for some of us kids who liked things a bit spicier! I made this dish quite a bit during college, and everyone always wanted more.

8-oz. pkg. medium egg noodles, uncooked
2 6-oz. cans tuna, drained
10¾-oz. can cream of mushroom soup
1½ c. shredded Pepper Jack cheese
4-oz. can sliced mushrooms, drained
3 green onions, sliced
hot pepper sauce to taste
1½ c. potato chips, crushed and divided

Cook noodles according to package directions; drain. Meanwhile, mix remaining ingredients together in a bowl, reserving ½ cup crushed potato chips for topping. Mix in cooked noodles. Spread mixture into a greased 9"x9" baking pan; top with reserved chips. Bake, uncovered, at 350 degrees for 30 to 40 minutes, until hot and bubbly. Serves 4.

Elizabeth Kolberg
Tolland, CT

toss-ins for a twist

For something a little different, substitute 2 cups shredded cooked chicken for the tuna and crushed nacho cheese chips for the potato chips.

hot meal on the go!

Keep your dinner piping hot to enjoy at picnics, family reunions or a day out on the lake. Just line a cooler with aluminum foil and take it anywhere.

Seafood Chowder

I found this recipe in an old cookbook I bought at a book sale at our local library! I usually make biscuits to serve with it.

1 t. oil
1 c. onion, chopped
½ t. garlic powder
10¾-oz. can cream of celery soup
10¾-oz. can cream of potato soup

1¾ c. milk
½ lb. medium shrimp, peeled
½ lb. firm white fish fillet, cubed
1 t. fresh dill weed, chopped

"If company is coming, I like to add some crabmeat and asparagus to the chowder."

—Roberta

Heat oil in a large saucepan over medium heat; add onion and garlic powder. Cook until onion is tender; drain. Stir in soups and milk. Heat to a boil, stirring often. Add shrimp and fish. Cook over low heat for about 5 minutes, stirring occasionally, until shrimp turns pink and fish flakes easily. Stir in dill weed before serving. Serves 4.

Roberta Simpkins
Mentor-on-the-Lake, OH

Grilled Veggies &
Sausage, page 58

farmers' market favorites

Did you find a bushel of fresh veggies from the market and don't know what to make with them? Look no further than this collection of farm-stand recipes chock-full of garden goodness. With favorites such as Garden Mini Meatloaves (page 51), Veggie Pizza Casserole (page 52) and Vegetable Pot Pie (page 70), your family will love to eat their vegetables!

Veggie Hodgepodge

"I could eat this dish two or three times a week! The sausage and garlic give the veggies an incredible flavor. It's a fine way to get everyone to enjoy eating more vegetables."

—Shelly

1 to 2 T. olive oil
2 to 3 boneless, skinless
　chicken breasts, cooked and
　cubed
1 to 2 andouille or Kielbasa
　sausage links, sliced
1 to 2 sweet potatoes, peeled
　and cubed
1 bunch broccoli, cut into
　flowerets

½ head cauliflower, cut into
　flowerets
1 lb. green beans, cut up
1 zucchini, sliced
1 yellow squash, sliced
1 onion, sliced
4 t. garlic, minced
salt and pepper to taste

Spread oil in the bottom of a 13"x9" baking pan; set aside. Combine remaining ingredients in a large bowl. Toss to mix, spreading garlic, salt and pepper throughout. Spoon into pan; cover with aluminum foil. Bake at 350 degrees for one to 1½ hours, until vegetables are tender. Serves 8.

Shelly Wallace
Troy, IL

Barbecue Chicken Kabobs

Robin Hill (Rochester, NY)

4 boneless, skinless chicken
  breasts, cubed
1 green pepper, cut into 2-inch
  squares
1 sweet onion, cut into wedges

1 red pepper, cut into 2-inch
  squares
1 c. favorite barbecue sauce
Garnish: fresh rosemary sprigs

Thread chicken, green pepper, onion and red pepper pieces alternately onto skewers. Place kabobs on a lightly oiled grill over medium heat. Cook for 12 to 15 minutes, until juices run clear, turning and brushing frequently with barbecue sauce. Garnish with rosemary sprigs. Serves 4.

Grilled Tomato + Basil Chicken

A summertime favorite when spending time at the lake.

toss-ins for a twist

This delicious dinner is also yummy with pork chops instead of chicken.

8 plum tomatoes, divided
¾ c. balsamic vinegar
¼ c. fresh basil
2 T. olive oil
1 clove garlic, minced

½ t. salt
4 boneless, skinless chicken breasts
non-stick vegetable spray
Garnish: additional fresh basil

Cut 4 tomatoes into quarters and place in a food processor; add vinegar, basil, oil, garlic and salt. Cover and process until smooth. Pour ½ cup of tomato mixture into a small bowl; cover and refrigerate until serving. Pour remaining tomato mixture into a large plastic zipping bag; add chicken. Seal bag; turn to coat. Refrigerate for one hour; drain and discard marinade. Spray a grill rack with non-stick vegetable spray. Grill chicken, covered, over medium heat for 4 to 6 minutes on each side, until juices run clear. Cut remaining tomatoes in half; grill for 2 to 3 minutes on each side, until tender. Serve with chicken and reserved tomato mixture. Garnish with basil. Serves 4.

Vickie
Gooseberry Patch

Deb's Garden Bounty Dinner

You can also use chicken thighs, if you'd like.

1 T. oil
4 to 6 chicken legs
6 to 8 zucchini, chopped
1 lb. mushrooms, chopped
1 green pepper, chopped
1 red pepper, chopped
1 onion, chopped
2 14½-oz. cans stewed
  tomatoes

2 t. garlic, minced
1 t. turmeric
pepper to taste
cooked rice
Garnish: fresh parsley,
  chopped

toss-ins for a twist

This is great for lunch the next day, too. Simply shred the chicken and toss with veggies and rice.

Heat oil in a skillet over medium-high heat. Add chicken and cook 20 to 25 minutes, until golden. Set aside and keep warm. Add remaining ingredients except rice and garnish to skillet; cook 5 minutes. Return chicken to skillet and continue to cook until juices run clear. Serve with rice; garnish with parsley. Serves 4 to 6.

Deb Grumbine
Greeley, CO

Zucchini + Ratatouille Pasta

Jennifer Breeden (Chesterfield, VA)

2 T. olive oil
¾ lb. boneless, skinless chicken
   breasts, cut into ½-inch pieces
1 c. green pepper, sliced
1½ c. eggplant, peeled and diced

1½ c. zucchini, thinly sliced
27½-oz. jar pasta sauce
8-oz. pkg. penne pasta, cooked
Garnish: grated Parmesan cheese

Heat oil in a saucepan over medium-high heat; add chicken and green pepper. Cook until chicken is no longer pink, stirring frequently. Add eggplant and zucchini; cook 3 minutes, or until vegetables are tender, stirring frequently. Stir in pasta sauce and heat to boiling. Reduce heat and simmer, uncovered, 10 minutes, or until chicken juices run clear. Spoon sauce over pasta and garnish with grated Parmesan cheese. Serves 6.

Chicken Lo Mein

Super-simple to make and tastes terrific!

2 T. soy sauce
2 T. dry sherry or chicken broth
2 t. cornstarch
¾ lb. boneless, skinless chicken breasts or thighs, thinly sliced
8-oz. pkg. linguine pasta, uncooked
1 T. oil

1 T. toasted sesame oil
8-oz. pkg. sliced mushrooms
1 red or green pepper, cut into 2-inch strips
4 green onions, cut into 2-inch pieces
1½ c. snow peas
½ c. water
¼ t. chicken bouillon granules

Whisk together soy sauce, sherry or broth and cornstarch. Add chicken; stir to coat. Cover and refrigerate 30 minutes. Meanwhile, cook pasta according to package directions, omitting oil and salt, if called for. Drain well; set aside to keep warm. Add oils to a wok or skillet over medium-high heat. Stir-fry mushrooms, pepper and onions in hot oil for 2 minutes. Add snow peas; stir-fry one minute, or until vegetables are crisp-tender. Remove from skillet and set aside. Drain chicken, reserving marinade. Stir-fry chicken in same skillet for 2 to 3 minutes, until no longer pink. Push to sides of skillet. Combine water, bouillon and reserved marinade; pour into center of skillet. Bring to a boil; stir constantly, until mixture thickens. Add pasta and cooked vegetables; stir well. Continue to cook and stir until ingredients are heated through. Serves 4.

Jackie Valvardi
Haddon Heights, NJ

toss-ins for a twist

Add your favorite veggies to this Asian dish. Carrots, broccoli, cabbage and water chestnuts make great additions.

Pepper Steak

Freezing the beef roast for 30 minutes makes it easier to cut into thin strips.

supper in a snap

Make the dinnertime rush easier by prepping ahead of time. Slice the steak, peppers and celery and cut the tomatoes into wedges. When tummies are rumbling, this dish will come together before you can say lickety-split!

2-lb. boneless chuck roast, trimmed
5 T. olive oil, divided
¼ c. soy sauce
2 T. dry sherry or beef broth
1 t. ground ginger
½ t. sugar
1 green pepper, cut into strips
1 red pepper, cut into strips
1 onion, cut into 2-inch pieces

2 stalks celery, thinly sliced
¼ t. pepper
1 T. cornstarch
¾ c. beef broth
2 tomatoes, each cut into 8 wedges
cooked rice, polenta or gnocchi
Garnish: chopped fresh parsley

Cut roast across grain into ¹⁄₁₆-inch strips. Combine 2 tablespoons olive oil, soy sauce, sherry or broth, ginger and sugar in a large zipping bag. Seal bag; shake to blend. Add beef to bag; seal and turn to coat. Chill one hour. Remove beef from marinade, reserving marinade. Heat 2 tablespoons olive oil in a large skillet over medium-high heat. Increase heat to high. Add beef to skillet; cook 2 to 3 minutes, stirring often, until browned. Stir reserved marinade into beef; cover, reduce heat to low and simmer 17 to 20 minutes, until tender, stirring occasionally. Meanwhile, heat remaining one tablespoon olive oil in a large nonstick skillet over medium-high heat. Add peppers, onion, celery and pepper. Cook, stirring often, 3 to 4 minutes, until vegetables are crisp-tender. Remove from heat. Combine cornstarch and broth, stirring until smooth. Stir cornstarch mixture into beef mixture. Stir in vegetable mixture and tomatoes. Serve immediately over rice, polenta or gnocchi. Garnish with parsley. Serves 6.

dinner al fresco

Carry dinner outdoors to the backyard for a picnic. Use vintage pie tins as plates…serve up bottles of frosty root beer and red soda from an ice-filled bucket.

Beef + Snow Pea Stir-Fry

3 T. soy sauce
2 T. rice wine or rice vinegar
1 T. brown sugar, packed
½ t. cornstarch
1 T. oil
1 T. fresh ginger, peeled and
  minced
1 T. garlic, minced
1 lb. beef round steak, cut into
  thin strips
1 to 1½ c. snow peas
cooked rice

Combine soy sauce, rice wine or vinegar, brown sugar and cornstarch in a small bowl; set aside. Heat oil in a wok or skillet over medium-high heat. Add ginger and garlic and sauté for 30 seconds. Add steak and stir-fry for 2 minutes, or until evenly browned. Add snow peas and stir-fry for an additional 3 minutes. Add soy sauce mixture; bring to a boil, stirring constantly. Reduce heat and simmer until sauce is thick and smooth. Serve over rice. Serves 4.

Rhonda Reeder
Ellicott City, MD

Tasty Tostadas

1½ lbs. ground beef
1 onion, chopped
1 pkg. taco seasoning mix
oil
6 8-inch flour tortillas
1 15-oz. can kidney beans,
  rinsed and drained
1 tomato, chopped
1 8-oz. bag preshredded
  iceberg lettuce
1 avocado, peeled, pitted and
  chopped
2 c. shredded sharp Cheddar
  cheese
sour cream
salsa

Cook beef with onion and seasoning mix in a large skillet over medium heat; drain. Pour oil to a depth of ¼ inch into a heavy skillet. Fry tortillas, one at a time, in hot oil over high heat 20 seconds on each side, or until crisp and golden. Drain on paper towels. Layer beef mixture, beans, tomato, lettuce, avocado and cheese on warm tortillas. Serve with sour cream and salsa. Serves 6.

Garden Mini Meatloaves

I love to serve buttery mashed potatoes and green beans with these meatloaves.

1 c. dry bread crumbs, divided
1½ lbs. ground beef
1 egg, beaten
2 T. Worcestershire sauce
1 c. green, red or yellow pepper, grated
½ c. zucchini, grated
½ sweet onion, chopped
1 T. fresh thyme, minced
3 leaves fresh basil, minced
salt and pepper to taste
1 c. shredded Colby Jack cheese

"A terrific way to sneak in veggies for picky eaters!"
—Bethanna

Combine ½ cup bread crumbs and remaining ingredients except cheese in a large bowl; mix well. Divide mixture among 6 ungreased mini loaf pans or ramekins; sprinkle evenly with remaining bread crumbs. Set pans on a baking sheet. Bake, uncovered, at 400 degrees for 30 minutes. Using a turkey baster, drain off drippings. Sprinkle meatloaves evenly with cheese. Bake 5 more minutes, or until cheese melts. Serves 6.

Bethanna Kortie
Greer, SC

Veggie Pizza Casserole

A great way to serve up those zucchini that mysteriously appear on your doorstep in late summer…your family will never know that they're hidden in here!

2 to 4 c. zucchini, shredded
½ t. salt
2 eggs, beaten
½ c. grated Parmesan cheese
1 c. shredded Cheddar cheese, divided
2 c. shredded mozzarella cheese, divided
1 lb. ground beef
¾ c. sweet onion, chopped
15-oz. can tomato sauce
¼ t. dried oregano
¼ t. dried basil
½ t. garlic salt
1 T. fresh parsley, chopped
1 yellow or red pepper, chopped
¼ c. olives, sliced
Garnish: additional chopped fresh parsley

Place zucchini in a colander; sprinkle with salt and let drain well, squeezing out extra moisture. Place zucchini in a large bowl; stir in eggs, Parmesan cheese and half of each of the Cheddar and mozzarella cheeses. Spread into a greased 13"x9" baking pan. Bake, uncovered, at 400 degrees for 20 minutes. While baking, brown beef with onion in a skillet over medium heat; drain. Stir in tomato sauce and seasonings; heat through. Layer over baked zucchini; sprinkle with remaining cheeses. Arrange peppers and olives over top before serving; garnish with parsley. Serves 6 to 8.

Alona Webb
Edgerton, WI

toss-ins for a twist

Make Veggie Pizza Casserole with your favorite veggies. Try it with yellow squash, carrots or even eggplant. Just bake veggies in place of zucchini until tender and continue with the recipe as usual. It'll be a summertime favorite!

easy, breezy clean-up

Keep a can of non-stick vegetable spray near the stove… quickly spritz on a casserole dish or skillet for easy clean-up later.

Lillian's Slow-Cooker Beef Stew

Tapioca is used to thicken this comfort food dish. If you don't have any on hand, substitute an equal amount of flour.

2 lbs. stew beef cubes
2 potatoes, peeled and quartered
3 stalks celery, diced
4 carrots, peeled and thickly sliced
2 onions, quartered

2 c. cocktail vegetable juice
⅓ c. quick-cooking tapioca, uncooked
1 T. sugar
1 T. salt
½ t. dried basil
¼ t. pepper

Arrange beef and vegetables in a 5-quart slow cooker. Combine remaining ingredients; pour into slow cooker. Cover and cook on high setting one hour; reduce heat to low setting and cook 7 hours. Serves 8.

Nancy Dynes
Goose Creek, SC

Veggie-fied Taco Soup

"Our family loves tacos! I was looking for a more healthful way to enjoy this yummy dish, and I decided to play with the veggie content of a slow-cooker taco soup."

–Julie

1 lb. ground beef or turkey
½ yellow onion, finely chopped
2 carrots, peeled and finely chopped
2 stalks celery, finely chopped
10-oz. pkg. frozen corn or 1 ear yellow corn, kernels sliced off
15-oz. can black beans, drained and rinsed
14-oz. can chicken broth

8-oz. can tomato sauce
2¼ c. water
1-oz. pkg. ranch salad dressing mix
6 T. taco seasoning mix
Toppings: sour cream, shredded cheese, sliced green onions, diced tomatoes
Garnish: fresh cilantro, chopped

Cook beef or turkey in a skillet over medium heat for about 10 minutes, until browned; drain. Add onion, carrots and celery to skillet. Cook over medium-low heat for 5 to 6 minutes, until tender. Combine meat mixture and remaining ingredients except toppings and garnish in a slow cooker. Cover and cook on low setting for 4 to 6 hours. Serve with desired toppings. Garnish with cilantro. Serves 6 to 8.

Julie Dossantos
Fort Pierce, FL

Hearty Beef, Barley + Kale Soup

1 T. oil
1 lb. lean boneless beef roast, diced
⅔ to 1 c. onion, chopped
6 c. beef broth
2 c. carrots, peeled and diced

½ c. pearled barley, uncooked
1 t. dried thyme
Optional: ½ t. salt
1 lb. kale, trimmed and chopped
8-oz. pkg. sliced mushrooms

"This is my friend Josephine's favorite soup...sure to become one of your favorites, too!"

–Jane

Heat oil in a large heavy stockpot over medium-high heat. Add beef and onion; cook until beef is well browned. Drain; add broth, carrots, barley, thyme and salt, if using. Bring to a boil. Reduce heat; cover and simmer for one hour, or until beef and barley are tender. Meanwhile, in a steamer basket over boiling water, steam kale for 5 minutes, or until bright green; drain. Add kale and mushrooms to stockpot; return to a boil. Reduce heat; cover and simmer for another 5 to 10 minutes, until kale and mushrooms are tender. Serves 4 to 6.

Jane Hebert
Smithfield, RI

Tuscan Pork Loin

4-lb. boneless pork loin roast
8-oz. pkg. cream cheese, softened
1 T. dried pesto seasoning
½ c. baby spinach
6 slices bacon, crisply cooked
12-oz. jar roasted red peppers, drained and divided
1 t. paprika
1 t. salt
½ t. pepper
Garnish: baby spinach

Slice pork lengthwise, cutting down center, but not through other side. Open halves and cut down center of each half, cutting to, but not through other sides. Open pork into a rectangle. Place pork between 2 sheets of heavy-duty plastic wrap and flatten into an even thickness using a rolling pin or the flat side of a meat mallet.

Spread cream cheese evenly over pork. Sprinkle with pesto seasoning; arrange spinach over cream cheese. Top with bacon slices and half of red peppers; reserve remaining red peppers for another use. Roll up pork lengthwise; tie at 2-inch intervals with kitchen string. Rub pork with paprika, salt and pepper.

Place roast seam-side down on a lightly greased rack on an aluminum foil-lined baking sheet. Bake at 425 degrees for 30 minutes, or until a meat thermometer inserted into thickest portion registers 145 degrees. Remove from oven; let stand for 10 minutes. Remove string from pork; slice pork into ½-inch thick servings. Serve pork slices on a bed of spinach leaves, if desired. Serves 8 to 10.

Gina McClenning
Valrico, FL

Grilled Veggies & Sausage

Our family loves vegetables roasted in an aluminum foil pack on the grill, so I developed this main-dish meal we all enjoy. This can also be baked in a roasting pan in the oven at 350 degrees for about an hour.

1 lb. Kielbasa sausage, cut into bite-size pieces
4 to 5 redskin potatoes, cut into bite-size pieces
1 red onion, thinly sliced
1 zucchini, cut into 1-inch cubes
16-oz. pkg. baby carrots
1 yellow squash, cut into 1-inch cubes
non-stick vegetable spray
butter or olive oil to taste
salt, pepper, minced garlic, dried parsley and Italian seasoning to taste

Arrange sausage and vegetables on a large piece of heavy aluminum foil coated with non-stick vegetable spray. Dot with butter or drizzle with oil. Sprinkle with desired seasonings. Seal edges of foil tightly to create a pack. Place on a heated grill and cook for about one hour, until all vegetables are tender. Serves 6.

Cindy Edmondson
Red Creek, NY

fresh is best

As soon as you get home from the market, rinse fruits & veggies and then jot down menu ideas. That way, you'll enjoy them at their very freshest.

Rosemary's Layered Tomato-Pesto Bake

When my friend Rosemary found bunches of basil too good to pass up at the farmers' market, she made homemade pesto for this recipe. For convenience, I like to use store-bought pesto.

1 loaf **sourdough bread**, sliced
½-inch thick
non-stick vegetable spray
8-oz. pkg. **cream cheese**, cubed
8-oz. pkg. shredded **mozzarella cheese**
¾ c. **basil pesto sauce**

5-oz. pkg. **prosciutto** or **deli ham**, thinly sliced
1 lb. **tomatoes**, thinly sliced
5 **eggs**, beaten
1½ c. **half-and-half**
½ t. **salt**
pepper to taste

Arrange half the bread slices in a 2-quart casserole dish that has been sprayed with non-stick vegetable spray. Layer with half each of cream cheese, mozzarella, pesto, prosciutto or ham and tomatoes; repeat layering. Whisk together eggs, half-and-half, salt and pepper. Pour over layers; cover and chill for at least 2 hours or up to overnight. Remove from refrigerator 20 to 30 minutes before baking. Bake, uncovered, at 350 degrees for one hour, or until puffed, golden and lightly set in center. Let stand for 10 minutes. Run a knife along edges to loosen. Place a serving plate over top and carefully invert. Carefully invert again so that strata is right-side up. Serves 6.

Slow-Cooker Tortellini Harvest Soup

Kathi Noland (Lakewood, CO)

1 lb. Italian pork sausage links, browned and thinly sliced

1 onion, chopped

1 to 2 carrots, peeled and chopped

2 c. tomatoes, diced

2 14-oz. cans vegetable broth

14-oz. can pizza sauce

2 c. water

1 bay leaf

1 to 2 zucchini, shredded or sliced

9-oz. pkg. refrigerated cheese tortellini, uncooked

Combine all ingredients except zucchini and tortellini in a slow cooker. Cover and cook on low setting for 5 to 7 hours. Add zucchini and tortellini to slow cooker; cover and cook on low setting for one more hour. Discard bay leaf. Ladle into soup bowls. Serves 6.

Poblano Chowder

This is wonderful served with toasted Italian or French bread. I usually double the recipe and invite friends over to share it.

¾ c. all-purpose flour
½ c. plus 2 T. oil, divided
4 c. water
2 to 3 potatoes, peeled and diced
2 poblano peppers, diced
1 red onion, diced
8-oz. pkg. sliced mushrooms
1½ to 2 c. corn
3 tomatoes, diced

1 jalapeño pepper, diced
2 T. salt
1 T. pepper
1 T. garlic powder
4 c. whipping cream
1 c. fresh cilantro, finely chopped
Garnish: cooked shrimp, crab, sausage, chicken or beef

toss-ins for a twist

There are so many great varieties of peppers available at markets in the summer. Substitute your favorites for the poblanos, if you'd like.

In a small bowl, whisk flour and ½ cup oil together; set aside. In a saucepan, bring water to a boil. Whisking constantly, add flour mixture. Cook until slightly thickened. Reduce heat to low and simmer for 4 to 5 minutes. Remove from heat and set aside. In a large stockpot, heat remaining oil. Sauté vegetables for 20 minutes, or until potatoes are just tender; add seasonings. Gently stir in flour mixture to coat vegetables. Add cream and simmer until heated through. Stir in cilantro and garnish to taste. Serves 10.

Farm-Stand Ribollita

I've been making this soup for years & years, and it's one of our all-time favorites. Serve it hot, warm or cold…it tastes terrific no matter the temperature and is even better the next day.

2 T. butter
2 T. olive oil
1 onion, chopped
2 carrots, peeled and sliced
2 stalks celery, sliced
2 cloves garlic, minced
1 roasted red pepper, sliced

1 sprig fresh rosemary
2 c. chicken broth
1 zucchini, sliced
14½-oz. can diced tomatoes
Optional: 15½-oz. can
　　cannellini beans, drained
salt and pepper to taste

Melt butter with oil in a large stockpot over medium heat. Add onion and cook for about 10 minutes, until tender. Add carrots, celery and garlic. Reduce heat; cover and cook about 10 minutes, until vegetables are tender. Add red pepper and rosemary; cook 5 more minutes. Add broth, zucchini, tomatoes and beans, if desired. Simmer about 10 minutes, until zucchini is tender. Discard rosemary; season with salt and pepper to taste. To serve, float a Bread Crouton slice in each bowl of soup. Serves 8.

Bread Croutons:

8 slices French or Italian bread
1 clove garlic, halved

2 to 3 T. grated Parmesan cheese

Arrange bread slices on an ungreased baking sheet. Bake at 350 degrees for 4 to 5 minutes, until golden. Immediately rub garlic over each slice; sprinkle with cheese and return to oven just until cheese melts.

Tiffani Schulte
Wyandotte, MI

Cream of Wild Mushroom Soup

¼ c. butter
2 onions, chopped
4 cloves garlic, minced
6 stalks celery, cut into 1-inch pieces
2 lbs. assorted mushrooms, such as button, cremini, shiitake and chanterelle, stems removed
⅔ to 1 c. dried porcini mushrooms
6 c. chicken or vegetable broth
2 bay leaves
2 T. fresh thyme, coarsely chopped
8 to 10 peppercorns
2 t. kosher salt
¼ t. white pepper
2 c. whipping cream
Garnish: fresh thyme sprigs, crumbled goat cheese, croutons

"This is my grandmother's recipe. She used only button mushrooms, but now I've added a variety to update it a bit. Every time I smell this soup simmering, I still think of visiting her home."

–Amy

Melt butter in a stockpot over medium-high heat. Add onions and garlic; cook until almost tender. Add celery; cook for 5 minutes. Slice mushrooms and stir in; cook for 17 to 20 minutes, until liquid evaporates and mushrooms are almost tender. Add just enough broth to cover mushroom mixture. Enclose bay leaves, thyme and peppercorns in a large square of cheesecloth; tie with kitchen twine to make an herb bundle. Add herb bundle to soup; bring to a boil. Reduce heat to low. Cover and simmer for 30 minutes, or until mushrooms are soft. Discard herb bundle; stir in salt and white pepper. Stir in cream; heat thoroughly without boiling. Garnish as desired. Serves 8 to 10.

Amy Wrightsel
Louisville, KY

Iowa's Best Corn Chowder

Iowa is corn country, and this soup is a local favorite.

½ c. onion, diced
1 clove garlic, minced
½ t. ground cumin
1 t. olive oil
4 c. vegetable broth
4 c. corn
2 redskin potatoes, diced

½ t. kosher salt
⅛ t. pepper
¾ c. milk
1 t. fresh cilantro, chopped
Garnish: additional chopped
    fresh cilantro

Sauté onion, garlic and cumin in oil in a stockpot over medium heat for 5 minutes, or until onion is tender. Add broth and next 4 ingredients; bring to a boil. Reduce to a simmer and cook for 20 minutes, or until potatoes are tender. Add milk and cilantro; cook until thoroughly heated, stirring frequently. Garnish with additional chopped cilantro. Serves 8.

Kay Marone
Des Moines, IA

French Onion Soup

Robin Hill (Rochester, NY)

¼ c. butter
3 c. onion, sliced
1 T. sugar
1 t. salt
2 T. all-purpose flour

4 c. low-sodium beef broth
¼ c. dry white wine or beef broth
6 slices French bread
½ c. grated Parmesan cheese
½ c. shredded mozzarella cheese

Melt butter in a skillet over medium heat. Add onion; cook for 15 to 20 minutes, until soft. Stir in sugar and salt; continue to cook and stir until golden. Add flour; mix well. Combine onion mixture, broth and wine or broth in a 4-quart slow cooker. Cover and cook on high setting for 3 to 4 hours. Ladle soup into oven-proof bowls. Top with bread slices; sprinkle with cheeses. Broil one to 2 minutes, until cheese is bubbly and melted. Serves 6.

Smoky Hobo Dinner

Away from home all day? This delicious slow-cooker creation will have dinner waiting for you!

non-stick vegetable spray

5 potatoes, peeled and quartered

1 head cabbage, coarsely chopped

16-oz. pkg. baby carrots

1 onion, thickly sliced

salt and pepper to taste

14-oz. pkg. smoked pork sausage, sliced into 2-inch pieces

½ c. water

Spray a slow cooker with non-stick vegetable spray and add vegetables in layers, sprinkling each layer with salt and pepper to taste. Place sausage on top. Pour water down one side of slow cooker. Cover and cook on low setting for 6 to 8 hours. Serves 6.

Julie Pak
Henryetta, OK

Summer Risotto

Serve this fresh dish as a main course or as a side with grilled chicken or pork chops.

3 cloves garlic
2 shallots, chopped
3 T. olive oil, divided
2 c. Arborio rice
1 qt. vegetable broth, divided
1 lb. asparagus, chopped
3 plum tomatoes, diced

2 T. fresh basil, chopped
1½ c. corn
¾ c. fresh Parmesan cheese,
   grated and divided
salt and pepper to taste
zest of one lemon

supper in a snap

Many stores offer fresh-cut and pre-chopped veggies. They are a great time-saver and get dinner on the table quickly.

Sauté garlic and shallots in one tablespoon olive oil until tender; add rice and sauté 2 minutes. Add enough broth to cover rice; cook, stirring constantly, until broth is absorbed. Add remaining broth; heat 10 to 12 minutes, until rice is al dente. Add asparagus, tomatoes, basil and corn; stir in ½ cup Parmesan cheese and mix well. Season with salt and pepper to taste. Serve warm in a large bowl; toss with remaining olive oil, Parmesan cheese and lemon zest. Serves 2 as a main dish or 4 as a side dish.

Kathy Unruh
Fresno, CA

Vegetable Paella

Paella is one of the most famous Spanish dishes. Give it a try…you'll love it!

1 c. dried cannellini beans
1 c. dried lima beans
2 T. olive oil
1⅔ c. tomato, chopped
1 c. red pepper, chopped
1 c. yellow pepper, chopped
¾ c. onion, chopped
¾ c. zucchini, diced
¾ c. yellow squash, diced
1 T. fresh rosemary, chopped

2 cloves garlic, minced
3 14-oz. cans vegetable broth
⅔ c. water
⅓ c. sliced kalamata olives
½ t. saffron or turmeric
1 t. paprika
½ t. salt
¼ t. pepper
3 c. prepared wild rice

Sort and rinse beans; place in a large Dutch oven. Cover with water to 2 inches above beans; bring to a boil and cook 2 minutes. Remove from heat; cover and let stand one hour. Drain beans and set aside. Heat oil in a large Dutch oven over medium heat. Add tomato, red pepper, yellow pepper, onion, zucchini, squash, rosemary and garlic; sauté 5 minutes, or until tender. Add beans, broth, water, olives, saffron or turmeric, paprika, salt and pepper; cover. Reduce heat and simmer one hour, or until beans are tender. Stir in prepared rice and simmer an additional 3 minutes, or until heated through. Serves 6 to 8.

Tonya Sheppard
Galveston, TX

tasty treats

After a simple dinner, a sweet & easy dessert is in order. Place scoops of rainbow sherbet in parfait glasses and slip a fortune cookie over the edge of each glass…perfect!

Gnocchi + Vegetable Toss

Jennifer Patrick (Delaware, OH)

4 qts. water
17½-oz. pkg. potato gnocchi, uncooked
1 lb. asparagus, cut into bite-size pieces
1 zucchini, halved and sliced
1 yellow squash, halved and sliced
10-oz. pkg. grape tomatoes, halved
10-oz. jar sun-dried tomato-basil pesto sauce
½ c. sour cream

Bring 4 quarts of water to a boil in a stockpot. Add gnocchi and vegetables. Return to a boil; boil for 2 to 3 minutes, until gnocchi floats to top; drain. Mix pesto sauce with sour cream. Add to gnocchi mixture; toss until thoroughly coated. Serve hot or cold. Serves 4.

Vegetable Pot Pie

1 onion, chopped
8-oz. pkg. sliced mushrooms
1 clove garlic, minced
2 T. olive oil
2 carrots, peeled and diced
2 potatoes, peeled and diced
2 stalks celery, sliced
2 c. cauliflower flowerets
1 c. green beans, trimmed and
   snapped into ½-inch pieces

3 c. vegetable broth
1 t. kosher salt
1 t. pepper
2 T. cornstarch
2 T. soy sauce
¼ c. water
2 9-inch pie crusts

Cook onion, mushrooms and garlic in oil for 3 to 5 minutes, stirring frequently. Stir in remaining vegetables and broth. Bring to a boil; reduce heat and simmer. Cook about 5 minutes, or until vegetables are just tender. Season with salt and pepper. Combine cornstarch, soy sauce and water in a small bowl. Mix until cornstarch dissolves. Stir mixture into vegetables; simmer until sauce thickens. Roll out one crust and place in an ungreased 11"x7" baking pan. Spoon filling evenly over pastry. Roll out remaining crust and arrange over filling; crimp edges. Bake at 425 degrees for 30 minutes, or until crust is golden. Serves 6.

Megan Brooks
Antioch, TN

Italian Zucchini Casserole

Add some chopped cooked chicken to this casserole, if you'd like.

3 zucchini, sliced
3 T. olive oil, divided
1 onion, sliced
1 clove garlic, minced
28-oz. can diced tomatoes
1 T. fresh basil, minced
1½ t. fresh oregano, minced

½ t. garlic salt
¼ t. pepper
1½ c. favorite-flavor stuffing mix
½ c. grated Parmesan cheese
¾ c. shredded mozzarella cheese

Cook zucchini in one tablespoon oil in a skillet over medium heat 5 to 6 minutes, until tender. Drain and remove from skillet. Sauté onion and garlic in remaining oil for one minute. Add tomatoes and seasonings; simmer, uncovered, for 10 minutes. Remove from heat; gently stir in zucchini. Place in an ungreased 13"x9" baking dish. Top with stuffing mix; sprinkle with Parmesan cheese. Cover and bake at 350 degrees for 20 minutes. Uncover and sprinkle with mozzarella cheese; bake for 10 more minutes, or until cheese is bubbly and golden. Serves 6 to 8.

Jeanne Allen
Menomonie, WI

enjoy year 'round

Freeze this summer's fresh basil to enjoy all year long. Combine ¼ cup olive oil with 2 cups packed basil leaves in a food processor. Pulse until finely chopped, spoon into an ice-cube tray and freeze. Once the cubes are frozen, place them in a plastic freezer bag and return them to the freezer...they're great for flavoring soups, sauces and salad dressings.

Skillet Enchiladas,
page 86

sizzling skillet suppers

These stovetop sensations are ready in a jiffy! Whether you cook up Chicken Chimies (page 80), Country-Fried Steak (page 82), Italian Hamburger Mac (page 89) or Lemony Pork Piccata (page 90), everyone is sure to ask for seconds! And another bonus...you'll only have the skillet to clean!

Saucy Apple Barbecue Chicken

My five-year-old son requests this yummy chicken for dinner all the time!

supper in a snap

Serve this yummy chicken with refrigerated mashed sweet potatoes and steam-in-bag green beans...delicious!

4 boneless, skinless chicken breasts
½ t. pepper
1 T. olive oil
⅔ c. applesauce

⅔ c. spicy honey barbecue sauce
2 T. brown sugar, packed
1 t. chili powder

Sprinkle chicken with pepper. Cook chicken in oil in a large skillet over medium heat until golden on both sides but not cooked through. Combine remaining ingredients in a small bowl; spoon over chicken. Cover and cook 7 to 10 minutes longer, until chicken juices run clear. Serves 4.

Melissa Mishler
Columbia City, IN

Chicken Paprikash
Katie Conroy (Bethlehem, PA)

1 to 1½ lbs. boneless, skinless
   chicken breasts, chopped
¼ c. butter
1 onion, sliced
¼ c. water
1 cube chicken bouillon
1 T. paprika

1 t. salt
⅛ t. pepper
1 c. sour cream
12-oz. pkg. butter noodles, cooked
   and drained
Garnish: chopped fresh parsley

Brown chicken in butter in a large skillet over medium heat; add onion and cook for 5 minutes. Mix in remaining ingredients except sour cream, noodles and garnish; bring to a boil. Reduce heat; simmer, covered, for 30 minutes, stirring occasionally. Add sour cream when chicken juices run clear. Heat through without bringing to a boil; serve chicken and sauce over noodles. Garnish with parsley. Serves 4 to 6.

Citrus Chicken with Rice

Serve on toast, croissants or a bed of lettuce.

2 T. oil
3 boneless, skinless chicken breasts, chopped
½ c. mayonnaise-type salad dressing
½ c. orange juice

2 T. brown sugar, packed
1 c. cooked rice
1 green pepper, sliced
11-oz. can mandarin oranges
8-oz. can pineapple chunks, drained

Heat oil in a skillet over medium-high heat; add chicken. Sauté about 3 minutes, until chicken juices run clear; drain. Reduce heat to medium; stir in salad dressing, orange juice and brown sugar. Add rice and green pepper; bring to a boil. Remove from heat; fold in oranges and pineapple. Let stand, covered, for 5 minutes before serving. Serves 4.

Joyce Crider
Landisville, PA

Tropical Chicken Stir-Fry

This dish is so yummy and cooks up in a jiffy…it's a little taste of the islands! I like to serve scoops of orange sherbet and coconut ice cream for a sweet end to dinner.

¼ c. soy sauce
2 T. sugar
1 T. cider vinegar
1 T. catsup
1 T. garlic, minced
1 t. cornstarch
½ t. ground ginger
8-oz. can pineapple chunks, drained and ¼ c. juice reserved

2 T. oil
1 lb. boneless, skinless chicken breasts, sliced into strips
16-oz. pkg. frozen stir-fry vegetables, thawed
cooked rice
sliced almonds, toasted

Mix soy sauce, sugar, vinegar, catsup, garlic, cornstarch, ginger and reserved pineapple juice in a bowl; set aside. Heat oil in a skillet over medium-high heat. Add chicken; cook and stir for 5 minutes, or until chicken juices begin to run clear. Add vegetables; cook and stir for 4 minutes. Stir in pineapple chunks and soy sauce mixture; heat through. Serve over cooked rice; sprinkle with almonds. Serves 6.

Vickie
Gooseberry Patch

helpful hint

Slice stir-fry meat and veggies into equal-size pieces… they'll all be cooked to perfection at the same time.

Mouthwatering Chicken Quesadillas

"This is my husband's absolute favorite dish, and the ladies at work don't mind leftovers when I bring them! It's a huge crowd-pleaser and a favorite of just about everyone I know."

—Raegan

2 to 3 T. oil
6 to 8 boneless, skinless chicken breasts, cut into bite-size pieces
1 onion, diced
1 to 2 green peppers, diced
seasoning salt and pepper to taste
1⅓ c. water
2 1¼-oz. pkgs. taco seasoning mix
2 to 3 c. shredded Cheddar cheese
10 10-inch flour tortillas
non-stick vegetable spray
Optional: fresh cilantro, salsa, sliced jalapeño peppers

Heat oil in a large skillet over medium heat. Sauté chicken, onion, green peppers, salt and pepper until chicken juices run clear; drain. Add water and both packages of taco seasoning; simmer for 5 minutes. Add a sprinkle of cheese, some chicken mixture and another sprinkle of cheese on half of one tortilla. Repeat with remaining tortillas, cheese and chicken mixture. Lightly coat a large non-stick skillet with non-stick vegetable spray; heat over medium heat until hot. Place 2 quesadillas in skillet and cook 2 minutes on each side, or until heated through and edges are golden. Repeat with remaining quesadillas. Serve with your choice of toppings, if desired. Serves 6 to 8.

Raegan Caston
Charleston, WV

Grandma's Turkey à la King

This rich, creamy dish is so comforting!

½ c. sliced mushrooms
¼ c. butter
2 T. all-purpose flour
2 c. chicken broth
1 c. whipping cream

2 c. cooked turkey, cubed
⅔ c. frozen peas, thawed
salt and pepper to taste
6 to 8 frozen puff pastry
   shells, baked

supper in a snap

Have leftover biscuits from breakfast? Serve this delicious dish over biscuits instead of pastry shells. Rice is great too!

Sauté mushrooms in butter in a skillet over medium-low heat until tender. Stir in flour until smooth. Whisk in broth; cook and stir until slightly thickened. Stir in remaining ingredients except puff pastry shells. Reduce heat to low; cook until thickened. Spoon into pastry shells. Serves 6 to 8.

Kelly Alderson
Erie, PA

Chicken Chimies

Add a bit of heat to this Mexican favorite by using Pepper Jack cheese in place of regular Monterey Jack.

"Why go out to eat when this is just as good as any restaurant dish?"

—Diana

2 boneless, skinless chicken breasts, cooked and shredded
salt, pepper and garlic salt to taste
1 T. butter
10 8-inch flour tortillas
8-oz. pkg. shredded Monterey Jack cheese

6 green onions, diced
1 T. vegetable oil
Toppings: sour cream, guacamole, salsa
Optional: lettuce leaves

Sprinkle chicken with salt, pepper and garlic salt to taste. Heat butter in a large skillet over medium heat; add chicken and sauté about 3 minutes. Spoon chicken evenly onto tortillas. Top with cheese and green onions; fold up sides and roll up burrito-style. Heat oil in a large skillet over medium-high heat. Add rolled-up tortillas and sauté until golden. Serve with your choice of toppings over lettuce leaves, if desired. Serves 6 to 8.

Diana Duff
Cypress, CA

clever condiments!

When serving a Mexican meal with a trio of toppings, such as chimichangas, slice the tops off 3 bell peppers, rinse and remove seeds. Then fill one pepper with guacamole, one with sour cream and one with salsa. Cover with reserved tops and refrigerate until ready to serve. Works great for cookouts, too…fill the peppers with mustard, mayo and catsup.

Country-Fried Steak

Dana Thompson (Prospect, OH)

1½ c. all-purpose flour
1 t. paprika
1 T. salt
¼ t. pepper
2 lbs. beef cube steak, cut into
   8 pieces

1 c. milk
¼ c. oil
2.6-oz. pkg. country-style gravy
   mix, prepared

Combine flour, paprika, salt and pepper; set aside. Dip steak into milk and then into flour mixture, pressing to coat completely. Heat oil in a large skillet over medium heat; add steak, in batches, and cook 5 minutes on each side, or until golden and tender, adding additional oil as needed. Top with prepared gravy. Serves 8.

Beef Stroganoff

Stirring in the sour cream at the end gives the sauce its creamy tanginess.

1½-lb. boneless sirloin steak, trimmed
1 t. salt
2 T. olive oil, divided
2 T. butter
8-oz. pkg. fresh mushrooms, sliced
1¼ c. beef broth
1 T. Worcestershire sauce
2 t. Dijon mustard
2 T. all-purpose flour
8-oz. container sour cream
Hot cooked, buttered egg noodles
Garnish: chopped fresh parsley

Slice steak across the grain into 2- x ⅛-inch strips; sprinkle with salt. Heat one tablespoon oil in a large skillet over high heat. Add steak and cook until browned, turning once. Remove steak from skillet and keep warm. Melt butter with remaining one tablespoon oil in skillet over medium-high heat; add mushrooms, and cook 6 minutes, or until liquid is almost absorbed, stirring occasionally to loosen particles from bottom of skillet. Combine beef broth, Worcestershire sauce and mustard in a small bowl; whisk in flour. Add broth mixture to skillet; stir well. Reduce heat to medium and cook, stirring constantly, 6 minutes, or until thickened. Stir in steak. Reduce heat to medium-low; cover and cook 20 minutes, or until steak is tender. Just before serving, stir in sour cream; cook one minute, or just until thoroughly heated. Serve over hot egg noodles. Garnish with parsley. Serves 4 to 6.

supper in a snap

This dish can easily be made ahead and reheated. It's also great served with steamed broccoli. Make the broccoli fancy by stirring together some softened butter, salt, pepper and orange zest. Toss with the hot broccoli and dinner is done!

Tangy Beef Patties

These tasty little burgers used to be served at our cousins' parties when our children were small. The ingredients in the Special Sauce may seem surprising, but they combine very nicely.

1 c. soft bread crumbs
½ c. milk
2 eggs, beaten
2 lbs. ground beef

2 t. salt
1 t. dried minced onion
¼ t. pepper
Garnish: sliced green onions

Mix together all ingredients except garnish in a large bowl. Form into 10 to 12 silver dollar-size patties. Brown patties in a large skillet over medium heat; drain. Pour Special Sauce over patties and simmer, covered, for 30 minutes. Garnish with green onions. Serves 5 to 6.

Special Sauce:

1 c. chili sauce
¾ c. grape jelly
1 T. lemon juice

1 t. Worcestershire sauce
1 t. mustard

Mix together all ingredients in a bowl.

Carol Zillig
Lincoln, NE

supper in a snap

This is a great make-ahead dinner. Form the patties and prepare the sauce in advance and keep them chilled. Serve with roasted potatoes and a salad...yum!

specialty of the house

Whip up your own custom seasoning mix...try equal parts brown sugar, salt, pepper, garlic powder and paprika. Use for chicken, pork chops or hamburger patties...delicious and out of the ordinary!

County Fair Maidrites

1¼ lbs. ground beef
2 T. onion, diced
1½ t. salt
¼ t. pepper
1¼ c. catsup
1½ T. mustard

1 T. quick-cooking oats,
  uncooked
1½ t. brown sugar, packed
¼ t. Worcestershire sauce
4 hamburger buns, split

"For many years, my mom ran the 4-H food stand at our county fair. We waited all year long for Mom to start cooking these."

–Samantha

Brown ground beef in a large skillet over medium heat; drain. Add onion, salt and pepper; cook until onion is transparent. Add remaining ingredients except buns; stir and simmer until heated through. Spoon onto buns. Serves 4.

Samantha Moyer
Farragut, IA

Skillet Enchiladas

Try diced potatoes in place of ground beef for a vegetarian twist.

¼ c. oil
8 8-inch corn tortillas
3 c. shredded Cheddar cheese, divided

½ c. olives, chopped
Garnish: chopped fresh cilantro

Heat oil in a skillet; add one tortilla, heating just until softened. Remove from skillet and place onto paper towel; pat dry. Repeat with remaining tortillas. Fill tortillas evenly using 2½ cups cheese and olives; roll up and place seam-sides down in an electric or large non-stick skillet over medium heat. Pour Enchilada Sauce over the top; heat, covered, for 5 minutes. Sprinkle with remaining cheese; heat uncovered, until cheese melts. Garnish with cilantro. Serves 4.

Enchilada Sauce:

1 lb. ground beef
½ c. onion, chopped
2 T. chopped green chiles
⅓ c. milk

10¾-oz. can cream of mushroom soup
10-oz. can enchilada sauce

Brown beef with onion in a skillet over medium heat; drain. Stir in remaining ingredients; simmer for 20 to 25 minutes.

Julie Coles
Boise, ID

enchilada casserole!

Instead of rolling up tortillas enchilada style, just cut them into strips, layer the filling and sauce, and bake at 350° degrees until heated through.

Chinese-Style Skirt Steak

You really can enjoy your favorite take-out dinner at home…you won't believe how easy this is to make!

2 lbs. beef skirt or flank steak, thinly sliced
¼ c. oil
1 clove garlic, minced
1 t. salt
½ t. pepper
1 t. ground ginger
3 onions, sliced
3 green peppers, sliced
¼ c. cold water
½ c. soy sauce
1 t. sugar
½ c. beef broth
1 T. cornstarch
8-oz. can sliced water chestnuts, drained
8-oz. can sliced mushrooms, drained
cooked rice

toss-ins for a twist

This quick dinner is also great with chicken, pork or shrimp instead of steak. Try red or yellow peppers for added color.

Brown beef in oil in a skillet over medium-high heat. Sprinkle in seasonings. Spoon beef mixture into a bowl; set aside and keep warm. Add onions and peppers to skillet; cook 3 minutes. Return beef mixture to skillet; stir in remaining ingredients except rice and cook 2 minutes. Spoon over rice to serve. Serves 4 to 6.

Helen Adamson
Winthrop, MA

Beefy Tomato-Rice Skillet

1 lb. ground beef
1 c. celery, chopped
⅔ c. onion, chopped
½ c. green pepper, chopped
11-oz. can corn, drained
10¾-oz. can tomato soup

1 c. water
1 t. Italian seasoning
1 c. quick-cooking rice,
   uncooked
Garnish: chopped fresh parsley

Cook beef, celery, onion and green pepper in a skillet over medium heat, until meat is no longer pink and vegetables are tender; drain. Stir in corn, soup, water and Italian seasoning; bring to a boil. Stir in rice; cover and remove from heat. Let stand 10 minutes, or until rice is tender. Garnish with parsley. Serves 6.

Erin Brock
Charleston, WV

Italian Hamburger Mac

2 lbs. ground beef chuck
1 onion, diced
salt and pepper to taste
3 c. elbow macaroni, uncooked
2 46-oz. cans tomato juice

1 T. dried oregano
2 t. dried basil
1 t. garlic salt
1 t. onion salt
Garnish: fresh sage leaves

Cook beef in a skillet over medium heat until browned. Add onion, salt and pepper to taste. Continue cooking for 5 minutes; drain. Spoon beef mixture into a stockpot; add uncooked macaroni and remaining ingredients except garnish. Bring to a boil over medium-high heat. Reduce heat; cover and simmer for about 20 minutes, until macaroni is tender, stirring frequently. Remove from heat and cool 10 minutes before serving to allow mixture to thicken. Garnish with sage. Serves 8 to 10.

Ben Gothard
Jemison, AL

"When I was a kid, my mom always made a dish like this...I could just eat the entire potful. Now that I'm grown, I have put my own spin on the dish."

—Ben

Lemony Pork Piccata

Serve with pasta to enjoy every drop of the lemony sauce.

supper in a snap

These thin, tender pork slices cook up quick. While the pork cooks, have the pasta boiling. Serve with a spinach salad and yeast rolls to round out the meal.

1-lb. pork tenderloin, sliced into 8 portions
2 t. lemon-pepper seasoning
3 T. all-purpose flour
2 T. butter
¼ c. dry sherry or chicken broth
¼ c. lemon juice
¼ c. capers
4 to 6 thin slices lemon

Pound pork slices to ⅛-inch thickness, using a meat mallet or rolling pin. Lightly sprinkle pork with lemon-pepper seasoning and flour. Melt one tablespoon butter in a large skillet over medium-high heat. Add half of pork and sauté 2 to 3 minutes on each side until golden, turning once. Repeat procedure with remaining butter and pork. Place pork on a serving plate; set aside. Add sherry or chicken broth, lemon juice, capers and lemon slices to skillet. Cook 2 minutes, or until slightly thickened, scraping up browned bits. Add pork and heat through. Serves 4.

Melody Taynor
Everett, WA

dress it up!

Festive trimmings can turn even a plain meal into a feast. Pick up some inexpensive, brightly colored napkins and table coverings at the nearest dollar store, and you're already halfway to a party!

Creole Pork Chops & Rice

Creole Pork Chops + Rice

4 pork chops
1 T. oil
1 c. onion, diced
1 c. celery, diced
1 c. long-cooking rice,
  uncooked

29-oz. can tomato sauce
14½-oz. can diced tomatoes
salt and pepper to taste

Cook pork chops in oil in a skillet over medium heat until golden but not completely cooked. Stir in onion and remaining ingredients. Reduce heat to low. Cover and simmer 15 to 20 minutes, until rice is tender, adding more water as needed. Serves 4.

Phyllis Covington
Guthrie, KY

"This flavorful one-pot meal really smells amazing as it cooks... even the leftovers taste wonderful! It's yummy made with boneless, skinless chicken breasts instead of pork chops too."
—Phyllis

Pork + Pears

Pears and balsamic vinegar give this dish its kick.

3 T. butter, divided
2 pears, cored and thinly sliced
1 t. brown sugar, packed
4 1-inch-thick pork chops

1 T. all-purpose flour
1 c. chicken broth
1 T. balsamic vinegar

Melt one tablespoon butter in a skillet over medium heat; add pears and brown sugar. Stir occasionally, about 5 to 10 minutes, until tender; spoon into a bowl and set aside. Melt remaining butter in skillet; brown pork chops on both sides until completely cooked. Place pork chops on a platter; keep warm. Stir flour into drippings; gradually whisk in broth and balsamic vinegar and cook until thick and bubbly. Return pork chops to skillet; heat through. Serve pears over pork chops. Serves 4.

Theresa Jakab
Milford, CT

Ham Steak & Apple Skillet

Gail Prather (Hastings, NE)

3 T. butter
½ c. brown sugar, packed
1 T. Dijon mustard

2 c. apples, cored and diced
2 1-lb. bone-in ham steaks

Melt butter in a large skillet over medium heat. Add brown sugar and mustard; bring to a simmer. Add apples; cover and simmer for 5 minutes. Top apples with ham steaks. Cover with a lid; simmer for about 10 minutes, until apples are tender. Place ham on a platter and cut into serving-size pieces. Top ham with apples and sauce. Serves 6.

Asian-Style Pork + Noodles

My husband and I enjoy Chinese food, and I love to cook it at home…but it can be so much work! This recipe is quick & easy and a great way to use leftover pork. It's ready to eat in about 30 minutes, and it's scrumptious.

¾ c. orange juice
¼ c. dark hoisin sauce
3 T. cider vinegar
2 T. catsup
¾ t. coarse salt
8-oz. pkg. wide egg noodles, uncooked
1 bunch broccoli, separated into flowerets, stalks thinly sliced
½ lb. sugar snap peas or snow peas, trimmed
2 T. oil
1 lb. boneless pork loin, cut into ½-inch wide strips
3 T. cornstarch

Stir together orange juice, hoisin sauce, vinegar, catsup and salt in a small bowl; set aside. Cook noodles according to package directions just until tender, adding broccoli and peas during last minute of cooking. Drain; place in a large bowl. Meanwhile, heat oil in a large skillet over medium heat. Dredge pork in cornstarch, shaking off excess. Sauté pork until lightly golden and completely cooked, tossing frequently, about 3 minutes. Pour in orange juice mixture; stir and bring to a boil. Add pork mixture to noodle mixture; toss to combine. Serves 4.

Emily Pselos
Temecula, CA

noodle knowledge

A no-fuss way to cook egg noodles…bring water to a rolling boil and then turn off the heat. Add noodles; cover and let stand for 20 minutes, stirring twice. Perfect!

Sausage Orzo Skillet

Orzo is rice-shaped pasta and cooks up quick!

"This skillet meal is quick & easy, and my whole family likes it! I've tried several flavors of sausage, and they're all delicious."

—Julie

1 lb. ground pork sausage
14-oz. can beef broth
14½-oz. can stewed tomatoes, undrained

1¼ c. orzo pasta, uncooked
Optional: Italian seasoning to taste
Garnish: fresh basil leaves

Brown sausage in a skillet over medium heat; drain. Add broth and tomatoes with their juice; bring to a boil. Stir in orzo; sprinkle with Italian seasoning, if desired. Cover and simmer for 15 minutes, or until orzo is tender. Garnish with basil. Serves 4.

Julie Lundblad
Chardon, OH

Skillet Ham + Cheese
Kathy Hutchings (Lebanon, PA)

¼ c. onion, chopped
⅓ c. green pepper, chopped
¼ c. butter, melted
1 T. all-purpose flour
1 t. salt
3½ c. milk

2 c. cooked ham, cubed
8-oz. pkg. elbow macaroni, uncooked
1 c. sour cream
1 c. shredded Swiss cheese
Garnish: fresh parsley, chopped

Sauté onion and green pepper in butter in a skillet over medium heat until tender; stir in flour and salt. Gradually whisk in milk; add ham and uncooked macaroni. Bring mixture to a boil, stirring constantly; reduce heat and simmer for 15 minutes, or until macaroni is tender. Stir in sour cream and cheese. Cook until cheese melts; do not boil. Garnish with parsley. Serves 6.

Pizzeria Sausage Supper

1 lb. ground pork sausage
½ c. onion, chopped
¼ c. green pepper, chopped
2 T. all-purpose flour
16-oz. can diced tomatoes,
   undrained
4-oz. can mushroom stems &
   pieces, drained
1 t. fresh oregano, chopped
½ t. fresh basil, chopped
¼ t. garlic powder
⅛ t. pepper
Optional: 4-oz. pkg. sliced
   pepperoni
10-oz. tube refrigerated
   biscuits, quartered
2 c. shredded mozzarella
   cheese
Garnish: grated Parmesan
   cheese, fresh sage leaves

Brown sausage, onion and pepper in a large oven-proof skillet over
medium heat. Drain; sprinkle with flour. Add undrained tomatoes, mushrooms and seasonings; mix well. Simmer until hot and bubbly, stirring
until slightly thickened. Add pepperoni, if desired. Arrange biscuit quarters
over mixture in skillet. Sprinkle biscuit layer with mozzarella cheese. Bake,
uncovered, at 400 degrees for 12 to 16 minutes, until biscuits are golden.
Garnish with Parmesan cheese and sage. Serves 10.

Kay Jones
Cleburne, TX

"My children loved
pizza when they were
growing up, like most
kids do. When I came
across this recipe, I
added my own touches,
and they loved it
because it had all their
favorite pizza flavors.
Add a salad to this
easy dish, and you've
got a meal!"

—Kay

clean up quick!

Save time on kitchen clean-up...always use a splatter
screen when cooking in a skillet or Dutch oven.

Cajun Shrimp Curry

Whip up this yummy seafood dish and warm up your family's tummies.

½ c. butter
1 onion, diced
3 stalks celery, diced
1 green pepper, diced
2 10¾-oz. cans cream of
   celery soup
1 c. milk

2 lbs. shrimp, cleaned and
   cooked
salt, pepper and curry powder
   to taste
cooked rice
Garnish: fresh parsley leaves

Melt butter in a Dutch oven over medium heat; sauté onion, celery and green pepper until tender. Mix in soup and milk; heat through. Fold in shrimp; season with salt, pepper and curry powder. Simmer until heated through; spoon over warm rice. Garnish with parsley. Serves 4.

Ann Mathis
Biscoe, AR

Shrimp Scampi

Spoil your family a little! This dish seems so fancy, yet it is simple to make.

supper in a snap

Serve this with angel hair pasta, steamed asparagus and garlic bread for a memorable meal in minutes.

2 lbs. large shrimp, peeled and cleaned
½ c. butter
½ c. oil
2 T. white wine or lemon juice
¼ c. green onion, minced
¼ c. fresh parsley, minced
1 T. garlic, minced
1 t. salt
pepper to taste
Optional: lemon wedges

Place shrimp in a large bowl; set aside. Combine remaining ingredients except lemon wedges in a saucepan over medium-low heat. Cook for 3 to 4 minutes, until well blended, stirring often. Pour most of butter mixture over shrimp; toss to coat well. Arrange shrimp on a 15"x10" jelly-roll pan in a single layer. Broil 3 to 4 inches from heat for about 5 minutes. Place shrimp on a serving platter; drizzle with remaining butter mixture. Serve with lemon wedges, if desired. Serves 6.

Vickie
Gooseberry Patch

Jambalaya

This hearty dish is delicious served with cornbread.

1 onion, chopped
½ lb. turkey Kielbasa sausage, sliced
1 T. oil
½ c. instant rice, uncooked
4 c. water
2 cubes chicken bouillon
16-oz. can pinto beans
15-oz. can black beans
14½-oz. can diced tomatoes
½ t. dried oregano
½ t. dried thyme
½ t. pepper
2 t. Cajun seasoning
¼ lb. large shrimp, peeled, cleaned and cooked

Sauté onion and Kielbasa sausage in oil in a skillet over medium heat until onion is tender; add remaining ingredients. Bring to a boil; reduce heat and simmer 30 minutes. Serves 4.

Jann Manwell
La Grande, OR

family mealtime

Over dinner, ask your children to tell you about the books they're reading at school and return the favor by sharing books you loved as a child. You may find you have some favorites in common!

Parmesan Fish Sticks

Round out this seaworthy meal with a side of fish-shaped crackers!

2 eggs
2 T. water
salt and pepper to taste
1½ c. seasoned bread crumbs
3 T. Parmesan cheese

2 lbs. sole fillets, sliced into
   4"x2" sticks
¼ c. olive oil
Optional: lemon wedges

Beat together eggs, water, salt and pepper in a small bowl; set aside. Combine bread crumbs and Parmesan cheese in a shallow bowl. Dip fish sticks into egg mixture; dredge in bread crumbs. Heat oil in a large skillet over medium-high heat. Add fish; cook about 3 minutes per side, until golden. Drain on paper towels. Serve with lemon wedges and Homemade Tartar Sauce, if desired. Serves 6.

Wendy Jacobs
Idaho Falls, ID

Homemade Tartar Sauce:

You can whip up this fresh tartar sauce in a jiffy.

1 c. mayonnaise
2 T. dill pickles, chopped
2 T. green olives with
   pimentos, chopped
1 T. onion, grated

1 T. fresh parsley, chopped
1 T. capers
1 T. lime or lemon juice
¼ t. garlic salt

Combine all ingredients in a bowl; mix well. Cover and refrigerate until serving time. Makes about 1½ cups.

Barb Stout
Delaware, OH

Mom's Salmon Patties
Denise Frederick (Climax, NY)

My mom used to make these yummy salmon patties when I was a child. This recipe brings back such great memories!

14¾-oz. can salmon, drained and
   flaked
¼ c. onion, finely chopped
¼ c. cornmeal
¼ c. all-purpose flour

1 egg, beaten
3 T. mayonnaise
salt and pepper to taste
2 T. oil
Garnish: fresh dill weed

Combine all ingredients except oil and garnish in a bowl. Mix until well blended; form into 4 to 5 patties. Heat oil in a skillet over medium heat. Add patties and cook until golden on each side, turning only once because the patties are fragile. Drain on paper towels. Garnish with dill weed. Serves 4 to 5.

Linda's Spring Greens
Pizza, page 114

pronto pizza + pasta

Not sure what to have for dinner tonight? Don't go by the drive-thru...everyone loves pizza and pasta! From Mexican Pizza (page 107) and Mom's Veggie Pizza (page 113) to Italian 3-Cheese Stuffed Shells (page 120) and Aunt B's Chicken Tetrazzini (page 126), you'll discover new and old favorites to share with family & friends.

Deep-Dish Sausage Pizza

Why go out to a pizza parlor when you can feast on a hot, hearty pizza right from your own kitchen? It's chock-full of the great Italian sausage and sweet pepper flavors that we love.

16-oz. pkg. frozen bread dough, thawed

1 lb. sweet Italian pork sausage, casings removed

2½ c. shredded mozzarella cheese, divided

1 green pepper, cut into squares

1 red pepper, cut into squares

28-oz. can diced tomatoes, drained

¾ t. dried oregano

½ t. salt

¼ t. garlic powder

½ c. grated Parmesan cheese

Press thawed dough into the bottom and up the sides of a greased 13"x9" baking pan; set aside. Crumble sausage in a large skillet and cook until no longer pink; drain. Sprinkle sausage over dough; top with 2 cups mozzarella cheese. Sauté peppers in the same skillet until slightly tender. Stir in tomatoes and seasonings; spoon over pizza. Sprinkle with Parmesan cheese and remaining ½ cup mozzarella cheese. Bake, uncovered, at 350 degrees for 25 to 35 minutes, until crust is golden. Serves 8.

Kathleen Sturm
Corona, CA

party time!

A make-it-yourself pizza party is great for pizza-loving youngsters! It's cheaper than ordering from a pizza shop and doubles as a fun party activity. Set out ready-to-bake pizza crusts and lots of toppings and let party guests get creative.

Mexican Pizza
Beth Gladu (Grasonville, MD)

2 8-oz. tubes refrigerated crescent
  rolls
8-oz. container sour cream
2 T. taco seasoning mix
16-oz. can refried beans

1 c. lettuce, shredded
3 green onions, sliced
1 tomato, diced
1 green pepper, diced
1 c. shredded Cheddar cheese

Spread crescent rolls in a single layer on an ungreased baking sheet; pinch seams together. Bake at 375 degrees for 15 to 20 minutes, until lightly golden. Remove from oven; cool. Mix sour cream and taco seasoning in a bowl. Spread refried beans over rolls; top with sour cream mixture. Layer with lettuce, onions, tomato and green pepper; sprinkle with cheese. Cut into squares. Serves 6 to 8.

White Pizza KellyJean Gettelfinger (Sellersburg, IN)

When we purchase a deli roast chicken from our local store, I make this pizza with the left-overs. My children started calling it "white pizza" when they were little, and the name stuck.

6½-oz. pkg. pizza dough mix
1 c. Alfredo sauce
2 c. cooked chicken, shredded
½ c. bacon bits

Optional: additional toppings
    such as olives, mushrooms
    and capers
2 c. shredded mozzarella cheese

Prepare pizza dough and bake according to package directions. Remove from oven just as crust starts to turn golden. Spread sauce over top. Layer with chicken; sprinkle with bacon bits. Layer with additional toppings, if desired. Top with mozzarella cheese. Bake at 450 degrees for another 3 to 5 minutes, until cheese melts. Serves 4 to 6.

Topsy-Turvy Pizza

2 T. oil
½ lb. hot or mild ground
   pork sausage
1 lb. ground beef
1 onion, chopped
¾ t. garlic powder
¾ t. Italian seasoning
15-oz. can pizza sauce

8-oz. pkg. shredded mozzarella
   cheese
1½ c. all-purpose flour
¼ t. salt
2 eggs, beaten
1 c. milk
½ c. grated Parmesan cheese
Garnish: chopped fresh basil

"We have enjoyed this recipe for years while traveling in our RV."
–Ethel

Heat oil over medium heat in a cast-iron skillet. Add sausage, ground beef and onion. Cook until browned; drain. Add garlic powder, Italian seasoning and pizza sauce; stir well. Sprinkle with mozzarella cheese. Combine remaining ingredients except Parmesan cheese and garnish in a large bowl; mix well. Spread over meat mixture; sprinkle with Parmesan cheese. Bake at 400 degrees for 20 to 30 minutes, until golden. Garnish with basil. Serves 6 to 8.

Ethel Kight
Moorefield, WV

Greek Pizza

Greek Pizza

My husband and I love making this recipe in the summer. Every Saturday morning we go to the farmers' market to buy basil that's been freshly picked that same morning...a tradition we look forward to each summer.

1 c. basil pesto sauce
12-inch Italian pizza crust
1 c. shredded mozzarella cheese
1½ c. cooked chicken, diced
½ c. red onion, chopped
½ c. green pepper, chopped
¼ c. sliced black olives

Optional: ¼ c. sliced banana peppers
4-oz. package crumbled feta cheese
⅛ t. dried oregano
Garnish: fresh basil

Spread pesto on pizza crust; sprinkle with mozzarella cheese. Add chicken, onion, green pepper, black olives and banana peppers, if using; top with feta cheese and oregano. Bake at 450 degrees for 10 minutes, or until crust is golden and cheese melts. Garnish with basil. Serves 5 to 8.

Dawn Horton
Columbus, OH

supper in a snap

There are so many great salad mixes available at grocery stores. Choose your favorite to pair with pizza...so easy!

Garden-Fresh Pesto Pizza

With this easy pizza, you can really taste what summer is all about! I came up with this recipe last summer when I had a bounty of cherry tomatoes and fresh basil.

12-inch pizza crust
⅓ to ½ c. basil pesto sauce
2 c. shredded mozzarella cheese

1½ c. cherry tomatoes, halved
Optional: 4 leaves fresh basil

Place crust on a 12" pizza pan lightly greased with non-stick vegetable spray, if directed on package. Spread pesto over pizza crust and top with cheese. Scatter tomatoes over cheese; add a basil leaf to each quarter of the pizza, if desired. Bake at 425 degrees for about 8 to 10 minutes, until crust is crisp and cheese is lightly golden. Cut into wedges. Serves 8.

Jennifer Oglesby
Brookville, IN

Grilled Barbecue Chicken Pizza

The grill is not just for burgers anymore! For a smoky flavor and crispy crust, grilled pizza is the way to go.

13.8-oz. tube refrigerated pizza crust dough
⅔ c. barbecue sauce
2 boneless, skinless chicken breasts, cooked and cut into strips

8-oz. pkg. shredded mozzarella cheese
½ c. green onions, chopped

Spray a baking sheet with non-stick vegetable spray; roll dough into a 16"x12" rectangle. Spread sauce over dough; arrange cooked chicken strips on top. Sprinkle with shredded cheese. Spray cold grill rack with non-stick vegetable spray. Place baking sheet on grill rack; grill, covered, over medium-low heat (275 to 325 degrees) for 3 minutes, or until dough begins to set (is no longer doughy). Slide dough off baking sheet and onto grill rack; continue grilling, covered, 10 more minutes. Use baking sheet to remove pizza from grill rack; sprinkle with green onions. Slice into squares. Serves 4.

Phyllis Wittig
Quartz Hill, CA

simple sides

Toss together a cool, easy side for six…corn and tomato salad. Combine a drained can of corn, a drained can of diced tomatoes with sweet onions, 3 sliced green onions and ¼ cup chopped fresh parsley or cilantro. Add ⅓ cup lime juice, ⅓ cup seasoned rice vinegar and salt to taste. Pop in the refrigerator and chill until dinnertime.

Mom's Veggie Pizza

2 8-oz. tubes refrigerated
    crescent rolls
8-oz. pkg. cream cheese,
    softened
1-oz. pkg. ranch salad dressing
    mix

4 c. favorite vegetables, finely
    chopped, such as broccoli,
    carrots, lettuce, tomatoes,
    peppers and onions
8-oz. pkg. shredded Cheddar
    cheese

Unroll crescent rolls and press onto an ungreased 15"x10" jelly-roll pan. Bake according to package directions; cool. Combine cream cheese and ranch dressing mix; spread over crust. Top with vegetables and sprinkle with cheese; refrigerate until ready to serve. Serves 8.

Beckie Kreml
Peebles, OH

"My mom used to make this for church dinners and showers. Now I make it for our fellowship Sunday after evening service. It's easy to make, and there are never leftovers!"

—Beckie

Linda's Spring Greens Pizza

My sister told me she was bringing this pizza to my house for a get-together. A pizza topped with greens? I thought she was crazy! But it was really good… everyone liked it, and it is healthy too.

2 c. broccoli flowerets
11 spears asparagus, trimmed
12-inch whole-wheat Italian
   pizza crust
6-oz. pkg. baby spinach
1 c. grated Parmesan cheese
1 T. garlic, minced

1 t. salt
1 t. pepper
¼ c. chicken broth
1 T. oil
2 c. yellow onion, sliced
3½-oz. pkg. crumbled reduced-
   fat feta cheese

Steam broccoli and asparagus in a steamer basket over boiling water about 5 minutes, until crisp-tender. Drain well; set aside. Place pizza crust on a baking sheet. Bake at 450 degrees for 5 minutes, or until lightly golden; cool. Combine spinach, Parmesan cheese, garlic, salt and pepper in a food processor. Pulse until puréed, adding broth as needed for a smooth consistency; set aside. Heat oil in a large non-stick skillet over medium-high heat. Cook onion, stirring frequently, 4 to 5 minutes, until golden on edges. Spread spinach mixture on pizza crust. Arrange broccoli, asparagus and onion on pizza as desired. Top with feta cheese. Bake at 450 degrees for about 5 minutes, until toppings are hot. Cut into wedges. Serves 6 to 8.

Carolyn Deckard
Bedford, IN

garden goodness

Gardens turn up the best pizza toppers…try something new such as chopped spinach, green onions, chives, cilantro, asparagus, sliced roma tomatoes or shredded carrots.

Bruschetta Pizza

If you can, prepare the bruschetta mix early in the day. The longer the flavor blends, the better it tastes. You'll have some left over, but that's okay. I made an omelet with this mix, and it was awesome!

10 roma tomatoes, chopped
5 to 6 cloves garlic, minced
2 T. fresh basil, chopped
½ red onion, finely chopped
¼ c. plus 1 T. olive oil, divided
½ t. pepper
¼ t. garlic salt

¼ c. balsamic vinegar
13.8-oz. tube refrigerated
  pizza crust dough
½ c. pizza sauce
8-oz. pkg. shredded Italian-
  blend cheese
dried oregano to taste

supper in a snap

In a time crunch? The bruschetta topping can be made ahead. Or buy prepared bruschetta found in the deli department at the grocery store.

Combine tomatoes, garlic, basil, onion, ¼ c. oil, pepper, garlic salt and vinegar in a large bowl. Stir to blend, Place pizza crust dough on an ungreased baking sheet. Spread with pizza sauce. Top with 1½ to 2 cups tomato mixture. Sprinkle with cheese and oregano. Drizzle remaining oil over top. Bake according to pizza crust dough package directions. Serves 6.

Madonna Alexander
Chicago, IL

Veggie Mini Pizzas
Elisha Wiggins (Suwanee, GA)

The taste of juicy summertime tomatoes and fresh spinach is unbeatable on these yummy mini pizzas.

6 pita rounds
1½ c. pizza or pasta sauce
1 c. baby spinach
2 plum tomatoes, sliced

8-oz. pkg. shredded mozzarella cheese
1 T. olive oil

Place pita rounds on an ungreased baking sheet. Spread each with ¼ cup sauce; top with spinach, tomato and cheese. Drizzle each pita with ½ teaspoon oil. Bake at 350 degrees for 15 to 20 minutes, until cheese is bubbly. Serves 6.

Poppy's Onion Pizza

For a light vegetarian dinner, this pizza is the best choice.

3 T. olive oil, divided
10-inch refrigerated pizza crust
2 onions, diced
garlic powder to taste

paprika to taste
Optional: salt and pepper to taste

"My dad became a wonderful cook when he retired...he passed this traditional Italian recipe on to me."
—Lisa

Lightly coat pizza pan with one tablespoon olive oil; place pizza crust into pan. Coat with one tablespoon olive oil; set aside. Sauté onions in remaining olive oil until golden; spread evenly over pizza crust, lightly pressing down. Sprinkle with garlic powder and paprika; add salt and pepper to taste, if desired. Bake at 425 degrees for 20 minutes, or until golden. Serves 8.

Lisa Arning
Garden City, NY

Quick + Easy Lasagna

Try this extra-cheesy lasagna...it's a winner!

toss-ins for a twist

Sneak some cooked spinach into this classic lasagna. Everyone will love it!

1 lb. ground beef, browned
2 24-oz. jars pasta sauce
16-oz. pkg. lasagna noodles, cooked and divided
2 c. ricotta cheese, divided
16-oz. pkg. shredded mozzarella cheese, divided

Mix together ground beef and pasta sauce; set aside. Spread one cup pasta sauce mixture on the bottom of an ungreased 13"x9" baking pan; layer with about half the noodles. Pour half the sauce on top; spoon half the ricotta cheese by spoonfuls onto the sauce. Sprinkle with half the mozzarella cheese; repeat layers, beginning with noodles. Bake, uncovered, at 350 degrees for 30 to 35 minutes, until cheese melts. Serves 12.

Tina Stuart
Scottsdale, AZ

Creamy Chicken Lasagna

This simple, special lasagna has a wonderful flavor that everyone loves.

2 to 3 c. cooked chicken, diced
10¾-oz. can cream of chicken soup
10¾-oz. can cream of mushroom soup
½ c. grated Parmesan cheese
8-oz. pkg. shredded mozzarella cheese, divided
8-oz. container sour cream
1 c. onion, finely chopped
1 c. sliced mushrooms
Optional: ¼ c. chopped pimento
½ t. garlic powder
6 to 9 lasagna noodles, cooked
Garnish: fresh parsley leaves

Combine chicken, soups, Parmesan cheese, ½ cup mozzarella cheese, sour cream, onion, mushrooms, pimento, if using, and garlic powder; mix well. Layer half of chicken mixture and half of lasagna noodles in a lightly greased 13"x9" baking pan. Repeat layers; sprinkle with remaining mozzarella. Bake, uncovered, at 350 degrees for 40 to 45 minutes. Let stand 5 to 10 minutes before serving. Garnish with parsley. Serves 6 to 8.

Kristi Root
Millersburg, OH

Quick & Easy Lasagna

Italian 3-Cheese Stuffed Shells

Stuffed pasta shells have never been as good as these, which are filled with three types of cheese and zesty Italian flavors.

1 lb. ground beef
1 c. onion, chopped
1 clove garlic, minced
2 c. hot water
12-oz. can tomato paste
1 T. instant beef bouillon
   granules

1½ t. dried oregano
16-oz. container cottage cheese
8-oz. pkg. shredded mozzarella
   cheese, divided
½ c. grated Parmesan cheese
1 egg, beaten
24 jumbo pasta shells, cooked

Cook beef, onion and garlic in a large skillet over medium-high heat, stirring until beef crumbles and is no longer pink; drain. Stir in water, tomato paste, bouillon granules and oregano; simmer over medium heat about 30 minutes. Stir together cottage cheese, one cup mozzarella, Parmesan cheese and egg in a medium bowl; mix well. Stuff cooked shells with cheese mixture; arrange in a greased 13"x9" baking pan. Pour beef mixture over shells. Cover and bake at 350 degrees for 40 to 45 minutes. Uncover and sprinkle with remaining mozzarella cheese. Bake 5 more minutes, or until cheese melts. Serves 6 to 8.

Melanie McNew
Cameron, MO

"A super dish for any get-together, and it's so simple to whip up."
—Melanie

storage secret

If a recipe calls for just part of an onion, keep the remaining fresh for another use. Rub the cut side with butter, place in a plastic zipping bag and refrigerate.

Melinda's Mexican Manicotti

Melinda Magness (Hodgen, OK)

8-oz. pkg. manicotti shells,
  uncooked
1 lb. lean ground beef
1¼-oz. pkg. taco seasoning mix

¾ c. water
16-oz. jar mild or hot picante sauce
8-oz. pkg. shredded Mexican
  cheese blend

Cook pasta shells according to package directions; drain. While shells are cooking, brown beef in a skillet over medium heat; drain. Stir in taco seasoning mix and water; reduce heat and simmer for 5 minutes. Fill cooked shells with beef mixture using a small spoon. Arrange shells in a lightly greased 13"x9" baking pan. Spoon picante sauce over top; sprinkle with cheese. Bake, uncovered, at 350 degrees for 30 minutes, or until hot and bubbly. Serves 4.

Ravioli Casserole

Give frozen ravioli a flavor boost with extra spaghetti sauce and layers of three different cheeses. Once your family tastes this ravioli, there will be no more requests for the canned variety!

"Any stuffed pasta works well...try meat or cheese tortellini, too!"

—Donna

26-oz. jar spaghetti sauce, divided
25-oz. pkg. frozen cheese ravioli, cooked and divided

2 c. cottage cheese, divided
4 c. shredded mozzarella cheese, divided
¼ c. shredded Parmesan cheese

Spread ½ cup spaghetti sauce in a lightly greased 13"x9" baking dish; layer with half the ravioli. Pour 1¼ cups sauce over ravioli; top with one cup cottage cheese and 2 cups mozzarella cheese. Repeat layers; sprinkle with Parmesan cheese. Bake, uncovered, at 350 degrees for 40 minutes. Let stand 10 minutes before serving. Serves 6 to 8.

Donna Nowicki
Center City, MN

3-Cheese Spinach Rigatoni

One of the best parts of this dish is that it is on the table in less than 30 minutes.

16-oz. pkg. rigatoni pasta, uncooked
3 T. olive oil, divided
10-oz. pkg. frozen chopped spinach, thawed and drained
2 c. ricotta cheese
5 T. grated Parmesan cheese, divided
¾ t. salt
¼ t. pepper
Optional: ¼ t. nutmeg
1½ c. shredded fontina cheese, divided
Garnish: additional grated Parmesan cheese

Cook rigatoni according to package directions. Drain; toss with one tablespoon oil and place in a lightly greased 13"x9" baking pan. Combine spinach, ricotta and 3 tablespoons Parmesan in a food processor or blender; purée until smooth. Add salt, pepper and nutmeg, if desired, to spinach mixture. Stir half of fontina into spinach mixture. Pour spinach mixture over rigatoni; top with remaining fontina and Parmesan cheese. Drizzle with remaining oil. Cover and bake at 450 degrees for 15 to 20 minutes, until golden and heated through. Sprinkle with additional Parmesan cheese. Serves 4.

Audrey Lett
Newark, DE

toss-ins for a twist

Add chopped cooked chicken or cooked and crumbled Italian sausage to this cheesy bake.

simple salad dressing

A crisp green salad goes well with almost any comforting main dish. For a zippy lemon dressing, shake up ½ cup olive oil, ⅓ cup fresh lemon juice and a tablespoon of Dijon mustard in a small jar and chill; stir to blend before serving.

Renae's Taco Bake

1 lb. ground beef
1¼-oz. pkg. taco seasoning
  mix
15-oz. can tomato sauce
3 c. elbow macaroni, cooked

8-oz. container sour cream
1 c. shredded Cheddar cheese,
  divided
¼ c. grated Parmesan cheese
Garnish: chopped green onions

Brown beef in a skillet over medium heat; drain. Stir in seasoning
mix and tomato sauce. Bring to a boil and remove from heat. Combine
cooked macaroni, sour cream and ½ cup Cheddar cheese in a bowl. Spoon
macaroni mixture into a lightly greased 13"x9" baking pan. Top with beef
mixture and remaining cheeses. Bake, uncovered, at 350 degrees for
30 minutes, or until hot and bubbly. Garnish with green onions. Serves 6.

Renae Scheiderer
Beallsville, OH

Penne with Sausage + Cheese

1 lb. hot or mild ground Italian
  pork sausage
3 cloves garlic, chopped
24-oz. jar marinara sauce with
  Cabernet and herbs
½ t. red pepper flakes
½ t. salt

½ t. pepper
12-oz. pkg. penne pasta, cooked
1 c. shredded mozzarella
  cheese
Garnish: grated Parmesan
  cheese, chopped fresh
  parsley

Cook sausage in a skillet over medium heat until browned; drain. Return
sausage to pan. Add garlic and cook about 2 minutes, until tender. Stir in
sauce and seasonings. Stir sauce mixture into cooked pasta; pour mixture
into a greased 12"x8" baking pan. Top with mozzarella cheese. Bake,
covered, at 375 degrees for 25 to 30 minutes, until bubbly and cheese
melts. Remove from oven; garnish with Parmesan cheese and parsley.
Serves 6.

Bev Bornheimer
Lyons, NY

Renae's Taco Bake

Aunt B's Chicken Tetrazzini

This makes two large trays of cheesy, chicken-y pasta...perfect for any church gathering when a covered dish is requested.

8 c. chicken broth

2 yellow onions, chopped

2 green peppers, chopped

16-oz. pkg. angel hair pasta, uncooked

2 lbs. boneless, skinless chicken breasts, cooked

2 4-oz. cans sliced mushrooms, drained

2 c. butter

1½ c. all-purpose flour

4 c. milk

6 c. pasteurized process cheese spread, cubed

Garnish: bread crumbs, green onions, chopped

Simmer broth, onions and peppers in a large stockpot over medium heat until boiling. Add pasta and cook as directed; do not drain. Add chicken and mushrooms; set aside. Combine butter, flour, milk and cheese in a medium saucepan over medium-low heat. Cook and stir until thickened; add to broth mixture and combine well. Pour into two lightly greased deep 13"x9" baking pans and top with bread crumbs. Bake, uncovered, at 350 degrees for 30 minutes, or until hot and bubbly. Garnish with green onions. Serves about 12.

Bryna Dunlap
Muskogee, OK

tag sale treasure

Don't pass up large, old-fashioned enamelware at tag sales. They're just the right size for family-size portions of stew, soup and other favorites...and indispensible for simmering chicken & noodles.

Cajun Chicken Pasta

A very simple recipe that's big on taste!

3 to 4 boneless, skinless
   chicken breasts, cut into
   strips
2 t. Cajun seasoning
2 T. butter
8 slices green pepper
8 slices red pepper
4 mushrooms, sliced
2 green onions, sliced

2 c. whipping cream
¼ t. dried basil
¼ t. lemon pepper
¼ t. salt
⅛ t. garlic salt
⅛ t. pepper
8-oz. pkg. linguine, cooked
Garnish: grated Parmesan
   cheese, fresh basil leaves

Toss chicken with Cajun seasoning in a bowl. Sauté chicken in butter in a skillet over medium heat about 5 minutes, until juices run clear. Add peppers, mushrooms and onions; sauté for 2 to 3 minutes. Reduce heat; add cream and remaining seasonings. Heat through but do not boil. Toss with linguine or spoon over individual servings of linguine. Garnish with Parmesan cheese and basil. Serves 4 to 6.

Jennifer Boyer
Sidney, MT

supper in a snap

Broccolini is an easy side dish that goes great with Cajun Chicken Pasta. First, steam the Broccolini until tender and then sauté it in butter, lemon juice and red pepper flakes... it's so good!

Florence's Meatball
Surprise

Florence's Meatball Surprise

1 lb. lean ground beef
1 egg, beaten
1 onion, diced
½ green pepper, diced
salt and pepper to taste
2 10¾-oz. cans cream of
　mushroom soup
1¼ c. water
16-oz. container sour cream
7-oz. pkg. elbow macaroni,
　cooked
15¼-oz. can peas, drained

supper in a snap

Make the meatballs ahead of
time and freeze them. Just be
sure to thaw them completely
before stirring them into the
soup mixture.

Mix beef, egg, onion and green pepper in a medium bowl. Add salt and pepper to taste. Shape mixture into meatballs. Brown meatballs on all sides in a skillet over medium heat. Remove from skillet; drain. Blend together soup, water, sour cream and macaroni in a large bowl. Stir in meatballs and peas. Pour meatball mixture into a lightly greased 2-quart casserole dish. Bake, covered, at 350 degrees for 30 to 40 minutes. Serves 6 to 8.

Kim Watkins
Wagoner, OK

Hamburger-Noodle Bake

1 lb. ground beef
½ c. onion, chopped
2 8-oz. cans tomato sauce
1 T. sugar
¾ t. garlic salt
¼ t. pepper
1 c. cottage cheese
¼ c. sour cream
8-oz. pkg. cream cheese,
　softened
4 c. egg noodles, cooked
¼ c. grated Parmesan cheese
Garnish: chopped fresh
　parsley

Brown beef and onion in a skillet over medium heat; drain. Stir in tomato sauce, sugar, garlic salt and pepper; heat through. Set aside. Combine cottage cheese, sour cream and cream cheese in a bowl; gently stir in noodles. Spread half the cheese mixture in an ungreased 13"x9" baking pan. Layer with half the beef mixture; repeat layers. Sprinkle with Parmesan cheese. Bake, uncovered, at 350 degrees for 30 minutes. Garnish with parsley. Serves 8.

Kate Conroy
Bethlehem, PA

Easy Spaghetti + Meatballs

Stephanie Whisenhunt (Birmingham, AL)

12-oz. pkg. spaghetti, uncooked
24 frozen, cooked Italian-style
    meatballs, thawed
2 14½-oz. cans Italian-style diced
    tomatoes, undrained
2 6-oz. cans tomato paste

½ c. water
2 t. dried Italian seasoning
2 t. sugar
Optional: shredded Parmesan
    cheese

Cook pasta according to package directions; drain and keep warm. Meanwhile, add meatballs and next 5 ingredients to a Dutch oven. Cook over medium heat 20 minutes, stirring occasionally. Serve over hot cooked pasta. Sprinkle with Parmesan cheese, if desired. Serves 4 to 6.

Fresh Tomato & Basil Linguine

If ripe garden tomatoes are out of season, roma or cherry tomatoes make good substitutes.

1½ lbs. tomatoes, finely
    chopped
3 cloves garlic, minced
1 red pepper, chopped
1 bunch fresh basil, torn
½ c. olive oil

1 t. salt
¼ t. pepper
16-oz. pkg. linguine, cooked
Garnish: shredded Parmesan
    cheese

Stir together tomatoes, garlic, red pepper and basil in a large bowl; drizzle with oil. Sprinkle with salt and pepper; mix well and toss with hot cooked linguine. Sprinkle with Parmesan cheese, if desired. Serves 6 to 8.

Vickie
Gooseberry Patch

toss-ins for a twist

Make this meal extra-hearty by stirring in chopped cooked chicken, cooked shrimp, steamed clams or even your favorite cooked veggies.

Zippy Clam Linguine

For a richer, thicker sauce, stir in a little whipping cream.

2 green onions, chopped
3 cloves garlic, chopped
¼ c. olive oil divided
¼ c. butter or margarine
1 pt. cherry tomatoes, chopped
½ t. hot pepper sauce
½ t. Italian herb seasoning

2 6½-oz. cans minced clams, drained
16-oz. pkg. linguine, cooked and drained
Garnish: freshly grated Parmesan cheese

Sauté green onions and garlic in 2 tablespoons oil until tender; add remaining oil, butter or margarine, tomatoes, hot pepper sauce and Italian seasoning. Reduce heat and simmer until tomatoes cook down; add clams. Heat through; pour over pasta. Sprinkle with Parmesan cheese. Serves 6.

Vicki Hughes
Joliet, MT

Vermicelli with Shrimp

No shrimp on hand? Cooked chicken works well in this recipe too!

12-oz. pkg. vermicelli pasta
1 onion, chopped
2 T. oil
2 cloves garlic, minced
16-oz. can crushed tomatoes
  in thick purée

¼ t. red pepper flakes
¾ t. salt
1 lb. large shrimp, peeled,
  cleaned and cooked
Garnish: fresh basil leaves

Prepare pasta according to package directions; drain and keep warm. Sauté onion in oil in a skillet over medium heat about 5 minutes, until tender. Add garlic, stirring 30 seconds more. Mix in tomatoes, red pepper flakes and salt; reduce heat and simmer for 10 minutes. Add shrimp and cook about 4 minutes, stirring until heated through. Pour sauce over warm pasta; stir gently to mix. Garnish with basil. Serves 4 to 6.

Kim Gludt
Anaheim, CA

Thai Peanut Noodles

Not a shrimp lover? Substitute chicken breasts instead.

1 lb. large shrimp, peeled, cleaned and cooked
1 c. light Italian salad dressing, divided
8-oz. pkg. angel hair pasta
2 T. crunchy peanut butter
1 T. soy sauce
1 T. honey
1 t. ground ginger
½ t. red pepper flakes
1 carrot, peeled and shredded
1 c. green onions, chopped
1 T. sesame oil
2 T. fresh cilantro, chopped
Optional: ⅔ c. chopped peanuts

Coat shrimp with ½ cup salad dressing; refrigerate for 30 minutes. Meanwhile, prepare pasta according to package directions; drain. Whisk peanut butter with remaining salad dressing, soy sauce, honey, ginger and red pepper flakes in a bowl until smooth; set aside. Sauté carrot and green onions in sesame oil in a skillet over medium heat about 5 minutes; place in a large serving bowl. Add pasta, peanut butter mixture and shrimp; toss well. Sprinkle with cilantro and peanuts, if desired. Serves 4.

Emily Selmer
Sumner, WA

time-saving trick

Need to chop nuts in a hurry? Place them in a plastic zipping bag and roll with a rolling pin...so easy!

Fettuccine with Smoked Salmon

Fresh asparagus and dill weed pair up with creamy fettuccine and smoked salmon for a refreshing springtime meal.

8-oz. pkg. fettuccine, uncooked
1 lb. asparagus, cut into
   ½-inch pieces
1 c. whipping cream
2 T. fresh dill weed, chopped
1 T. prepared horseradish

4 oz. smoked salmon, cut into
   ½-inch pieces
½ t. salt
¼ t. pepper
freshly squeezed lemon juice

"I like to serve this spooned into a serving bowl ringed with fresh lettuce leaves."

—Carole

Cook pasta according to package directions; add asparagus during last 3 minutes of cooking time. Drain and set aside. Heat cream, dill weed and horseradish in a skillet over low heat about one minute, until hot; add pasta mixture, tossing to mix. Gently toss in salmon; add salt and pepper. Squeeze lemon juice over top. Serves 4 to 6.

Carole Larkins
Elmendorf Air Force Base, AK

Anytime Tortellini

A dish you really can enjoy anytime…either for lunch or dinner. For a lighter meal, use angel hair pasta in place of the tortellini.

1 T. olive oil
2 boneless, skinless chicken breasts
1 t. Montreal seasoning for chicken, divided
1 lb. asparagus, sliced into 1-inch pieces
1 portabella mushroom cap, chopped
6 sun-dried tomatoes, minced
1 T. dried parsley
salt to taste

1 T. Italian seasoning
1 c. white zinfandel wine or chicken broth
2 16-oz. pkgs. cheese or meat tortellini, uncooked
2 14½-oz. cans diced tomatoes with roasted garlic, undrained
½ c. chicken broth
Garnish: grated Parmesan cheese

Heat oil in a skillet over medium heat. Add chicken; sprinkle with ½ teaspoon Montreal seasoning. Stir-fry chicken until lightly golden. Stir in asparagus, mushroom and tomatoes; sprinkle with remaining Montreal seasoning, parsley, salt to taste and Italian seasoning. Stir and cook 6 minutes. Pour in wine or chicken broth and simmer. Meanwhile, cook tortellini according to package directions. Add tomatoes with juice and asparagus mixture. Simmer 7 minutes, slowly add ½ cup chicken broth and continue to simmer for 8 more minutes. When tortellini is done, drain and place in a large serving bowl. Top with chicken and asparagus mixture; garnish with Parmesan cheese. Serves 6.

Patricia Guerard
Hillsborough, NJ

Best Friends' Greek Pasta
Rachel Hill (Center, TX)

My best friend and I went to an Italian restaurant and ordered the Greek Pasta. We loved it so much that my friend went home and figured out how to make it. She passed this recipe on to me, and now every time I make it for socials, everyone wants the recipe.

3 to 4 chicken breast fillets
Cajun seasoning to taste
16-oz. pkg. penne pasta, cooked
¼ c. basil pesto sauce
2 T. garlic, minced

6-oz. jar pitted Kalamata olives, drained
8-oz. pkg. crumbled feta cheese
¾ c. Italian salad dressing

Sprinkle chicken with seasoning. Grill until juices run clear; slice into bite-size pieces and set aside. While pasta is still hot, stir in pesto and garlic; mix well. Stir in chicken, olives and cheese. Add salad dressing to coat; mix well. Serves 4 to 6.

Mediterranean Beef
Salad, page 157

speedy sandwiches + salads

You will always get supper on the table in no time with this classic combo. Everyone will gobble up the Ranch BLT Wraps paired with Pepper & Corn Salad (page 143). Or try Henderson Family Gyros (page 147). Craving a burger? Dagwood Burgers (page 148) are just the ticket. Serve with some simple baked home fries...yum!

Cobb Sandwiches
Joyce Chizauskie (Vacaville, CA)

If you don't have time to fry bacon, mix bacon bits with the blue cheese dressing.

2 T. blue cheese salad dressing
3 slices bread, toasted
4-oz. grilled boneless, skinless
   chicken breast
1 leaf green leaf lettuce

2 slices tomato
3 slices avocado
1 slice red onion
3 slices bacon, crisply cooked

Spread blue cheese salad dressing on one side of each slice of toasted bread. Place chicken breast on dressing side of first slice of bread; top with a second bread slice. Layer on lettuce, tomato, avocado, onion and bacon; top with remaining bread slice. Cut sandwich in quarters, securing each section with a toothpick. Makes 4 sandwich wedges.

Raspberry-Dijon Baguettes

These hearty sandwiches are perfect to take along on a picnic!

1 baguette, cut into 4 pieces
and halved horizontally
Dijon mustard to taste
raspberry jam to taste

4 boneless, skinless chicken
breasts, grilled and sliced
2 c. arugula leaves
Optional: red onion slices

Spread 4 slices of baguette with mustard. Top remaining slices with raspberry jam. Arrange a layer of grilled chicken over mustard; top with arugula and onion, if desired. Top with remaining baguette slices. Makes 4 sandwiches.

"A friend shared a similar recipe using roast beef...this is my spin on that recipe using grilled chicken."
—Deborah

Deborah Lomax
Peoria, IL

7-Fruit Salad

The soothing taste of this chilled fruit salad makes it a welcome treat during the heat of summer.

½ c. lime juice
½ c. water
½ c. sugar
2 nectarines, peeled and thinly
sliced
1 banana, thinly sliced
1 pt. blueberries

1 pt. strawberries, hulled and
sliced
1½ c. watermelon, scooped
into balls
1½ c. green grapes
1 kiwi, peeled and chopped

Whisk together lime juice, ½ cup water and sugar in a medium bowl until sugar dissolves; add nectarines and banana, stirring to coat. Combine blueberries, strawberries, watermelon, grapes and kiwi in a 2½-quart glass serving bowl; add nectarine mixture, gently tossing to mix. Cover and refrigerate for one hour. Serves 8 to 10.

Laurie Parks
Westerville, OH

Chicken Salad Croissants

This isn't your ordinary chicken salad...this version calls for raisins, almonds and dried cranberries.

2 c. cooked chicken, cubed
⅓ c. celery, diced
¼ c. raisins
¼ c. dried cranberries
¼ c. sliced almonds
⅔ c. mayonnaise
⅛ t. pepper

1 T. fresh parsley, minced
1 t. mustard
1 T. lemon juice
4 croissants, split in half horizontally
4 lettuce leaves

Combine chicken, celery, raisins, cranberries, almonds, mayonnaise, pepper, parsley, mustard and lemon juice in a large mixing bowl; mix well. Cover and refrigerate for 2 to 3 hours. Spoon about ¾ cup mixture on the bottom half of each croissant; add a lettuce leaf and the top croissant half. Makes 4 sandwiches.

Arlene Smulski
Lyons, IL

deli roast chicken

Pick up a roasted chicken at the deli for 2 meals in one. Serve it hot the first night and then slice or cube the rest to become the delicious start of a sandwich, soup or salad supper the next night.

Ranch BLT Wraps

For some festive Tex-Mex fun, use bandannas as napkins to serve with this wrap and salad.

6 leaves green leaf lettuce
6 sandwich wraps
12-oz. pkg. bacon, crisply cooked

1 lb. boneless, skinless chicken breasts, cooked and cubed
2 tomatoes, diced
ranch salad dressing to taste

Place one leaf lettuce on each sandwich wrap. Top with 2 to 3 slices bacon. Spoon chicken and tomatoes evenly over bacon. Drizzle with salad dressing and roll up. Makes 6 wraps.

Rachel Dingler
Howell, MI

"Our family loves to enjoy these wraps with a bowl of soup."

—Rachel

Pepper & Corn Salad

Toss in some cherry tomatoes, sliced cucumbers or any of your favorite summer veggies for a flavorful twist.

2 15¼-oz. cans corn, drained
1 bunch green onions, chopped
1 green pepper, chopped

5-oz. jar green olives with pimentos, drained and sliced
1 c. Italian salad dressing

Combine all ingredients in a serving bowl; cover and refrigerate overnight. Serves 6.

Lynn Newton
Oklahoma City, OK

All-American Sandwiches

Celebrate summer with these yummy sandwiches…the blue cheese is scrumptious!

1½ T. olive oil
2 red onions, thinly sliced
3½ T. red wine vinegar
6 c. arugula leaves, divided
¾ c. mayonnaise

salt and pepper to taste
4 ciabatta rolls, halved
¾ lb. thinly sliced smoked deli turkey
¾ c. crumbled blue cheese

Heat oil in a skillet over medium-high heat. Add onions and sauté until soft and lightly golden. Remove from heat and stir in vinegar. Set aside. Chop enough arugula to equal one cup. Stir in mayonnaise; season with salt and pepper to taste. Spread mayonnaise mixture over cut sides of rolls. Divide turkey evenly among bottom halves of rolls. Top with cheese, onion mixture, remaining arugula leaves and top halves of rolls. Makes 4 sandwiches.

Jo Ann
Gooseberry Patch

Marinated Broccoli Salad

So easy…you can mix it in a bag! Be sure to let the flavors blend overnight.

2 bunches broccoli flowerets, chopped
1 t. dill weed
¼ c. oil

¼ c. red wine vinegar
2 cloves garlic, minced
Optional: sweetened, dried cranberries; sliced almonds

Place broccoli, dill weed, oil, vinegar and garlic in a one-gallon plastic zipping bag; add cranberries and almonds, if using. Close bag and shake well. Refrigerate overnight, shaking occasionally; serve chilled. Serves 6.

Beverly Brown
Bowie, MD

Apricot-Cashew Salad Sandwiches

This sandwich is a great way to use leftover turkey.

2 c. cooked turkey, diced
1 Granny Smith apple, peeled, cored and diced
1 c. celery, chopped
¼ c. dried apricots, finely chopped
½ c. cashews, chopped
½ c. mayonnaise

¼ c. sour cream
2 T. apricot preserves
¼ t. ground ginger
⅛ t. nutmeg
⅛ t. pepper
8 slices sandwich bread
4 lettuce leaves

"So versatile...the kids enjoy this for lunch as a wrap or sandwich, but I've also served it over red leaf lettuce for a ladies' luncheon at church."

—Rhonda

Toss together turkey, apple, celery, apricots and cashews in a large bowl; set aside. Whisk together mayonnaise, sour cream, preserves, ginger, nutmeg and pepper in a separate bowl; spoon over turkey mixture and fold in until well blended. Spoon evenly onto 4 slices of bread. Top with a lettuce leaf and remaining bread slices. Makes 4 sandwiches.

Rhonda Reeder
Ellicott City, MD

Henderson Family Gyros

Be sure to marinate the meat for 6 to 12 hours. The result is worth it…meat that's tender and bursting with flavor!

¼ c. olive oil
¼ c. dry red wine or cranberry
  juice cocktail
Optional: 1 T. vinegar
4 cloves garlic, chopped
1 T. fresh oregano, chopped

2 lbs. pork or turkey
  tenderloin, thinly sliced
6 pita rounds, split
Garnish: baby spinach, red
  onion slices, tomato slices

Combine oil, wine or juice, vinegar, if using, garlic and oregano in a large plastic zipping bag. Add pork or turkey; seal and refrigerate for 6 to 12 hours. Line grill surface with a lightly greased piece of aluminum foil. Using a slotted spoon, remove meat mixture from plastic zipping bag and arrange on aluminum foil. Discard marinade. Grill over medium-high heat, turning meat slices until browned. Remove from grill. Toast pitas on grill until warmed. Spoon meat into pitas; drizzle with Cucumber Sauce. Top with desired amounts of spinach, red onion and tomato. Makes 6 gyros.

Cucumber Sauce:

¼ c. sour cream
¼ c. cucumber, peeled and
  diced
2 T. red onion, minced

¼ t. lemon pepper
¼ t. dried oregano
⅛ t. garlic powder

Combine all ingredients in a bowl. Chill until ready to serve.

Jessica Henderson
Bloomfield, IA

supper in a snap

These Greek wraps are the perfect make-ahead meal. Marinate the meat in the morning and make the sauce. Serve with some deli tabbouleh, and dinner's done!

Dagwood Burgers

Buns taste better toasted and won't get soggy. Lightly butter the buns and place them on a hot pan or grill for 30 seconds, or until toasted.

2 lbs. lean ground beef
1 lb. ground Italian pork sausage
2 c. dry bread crumbs
1 onion, chopped
½ c. barbecue sauce
1 egg, beaten

1.35-oz. pkg. onion soup mix
1 t. jalapeño pepper, seeded
  and diced
salt and pepper to taste
12 to 15 hamburger buns, split
Optional: lettuce leaf

Mix ground beef, pork, bread crumbs, onion, barbecue sauce, egg, onion soup mix and jalapeño in a very large bowl. Form into 12 to 15 patties; sprinkle with salt and pepper. Place on a grill or in a skillet over medium heat. Cook burgers to desired doneness; serve on buns. Garnish each serving with lettuce leaf, if desired. Makes 12 to 15 burgers.

Jennifer Scott
Checotah, OK

diner-themed dinner

A diner-themed dinner is fun for the whole family…make placemats from vintage maps, roll up flatware in paper napkins and serve catsup & mustard from plastic squeeze bottles.

Italian Sausage Sandwiches

The sausages are flavored with garlic and fennel seeds and are available sweet or hot. Let your taste buds lead you to your choice.

8 Italian sausages
1 Bermuda or Spanish onion, chopped
2 green peppers, quartered and sliced
1 t. salt
1 t. sugar
1 t. Italian seasoning
Optional: 2 tomatoes, chopped
8 hoagie rolls
4 t. butter, divided
16-oz. pkg. shredded mozzarella cheese

"This is a family favorite...there are never any leftovers."
–Joanne

Score the sausages every ½ inch. Cook sausages in a large skillet 15 minutes, or until browned and thoroughly cooked; place on paper towels. Drain, reserving 3 tablespoons drippings; return reserved drippings to skillet. Add onion to skillet and sauté until tender. Stir in green peppers, salt, sugar and Italian seasoning. Cover and cook for 5 minutes; stir in tomatoes, if desired. Place sausages on top. Cook, covered, for 5 minutes, or until mixture bubbles. Meanwhile, cut out center of rolls to make boat-shaped shells. Spread ½ teaspoon butter on the inside of each roll; place rolls on an ungreased baking sheet and bake at 350 degrees for 10 minutes. Place one sausage in each roll; top with onion mixture. Divide mozzarella cheese evenly among rolls. Makes 8 sandwiches.

Joanne Ciancio
Silver Lake, OH

Shrimply Wonderful Bagels

Serve on mini bagels for perfect bite-size sandwiches.

3-oz. pkg. cream cheese, softened
4¼-oz. can tiny shrimp, drained and rinsed
2 T. mayonnaise
1 T. lemon juice
½ t. dill weed
4 bagels, split and toasted
1 avocado, pitted, peeled and sliced

Combine cream cheese, shrimp, mayonnaise, lemon juice and dill weed; mix well. Spread mixture on 4 bagel halves. Top with avocado slices and remaining bagel halves. Makes 4 sandwiches.

Jennifer Gubbins
Homewood, IL

Dilly Cucumber Salad

4 c. cucumbers, peeled and thinly sliced
¾ c. sour cream
1 T. oil
1 t. sugar
½ t. garlic salt
½ t. salt
½ t. white vinegar
¼ t. dill weed

Place cucumbers in a serving dish. Mix sour cream, oil, sugar, garlic salt, salt and white vinegar in a separate bowl; add to cucumbers and toss to coat. Sprinkle dill weed over salad. Cover and refrigerate for at least one hour. Mix lightly before serving. Serves 5 to 6.

Debra Holme
Victoria, Australia

Dressed Oyster Po'boys

1¼ c. self-rising cornmeal mix
2 T. salt-free Creole seasoning
2 12-oz. containers fresh
   standard oysters, drained
peanut or vegetable oil
1 c. mayonnaise, divided
2 T. Dijon mustard
2 T. white vinegar

6 c. finely shredded
   multi-colored cabbage
2 T. catsup
1 T. prepared horseradish
1 t. salt-free Creole seasoning
¾ t. paprika
4 hoagie rolls, split and toasted

Combine cornmeal mix and Creole seasoning; dredge oysters in
mixture. Pour oil to a depth of 2 inches into a Dutch oven; heat to 375
degrees. Fry oysters, in 3 batches, 2 to 3 minutes, until golden. Place on
wire racks. Stir together ½ cup mayonnaise, mustard and vinegar. Stir in
cabbage; set slaw aside. Stir together remaining ½ cup mayonnaise, catsup,
horseradish, Creole seasoning and paprika. Spread bottom halves of rolls
with mayonnaise mixture. Layer with oysters and top with slaw; cover
with roll tops. Makes 4 sandwiches.

Extra-Cheesy Grilled Cheese

Delicious in winter with a steaming bowl of tomato soup…scrumptious in summer made with produce fresh from the garden!

¼ c. butter, softened
8 slices sourdough bread
4 slices provolone cheese
4 slices mozzarella cheese

Optional: 4 slices red onion,
  4 slices tomato, ¼ c. chopped
  fresh basil

Spread 1½ teaspoons butter on each of 8 bread slices. Place one bread slice, butter-side down, in a large skillet or on a hot griddle. Layer one slice provolone and one slice mozzarella cheese on bread slice. Top with an onion slice, tomato slice and one tablespoon basil, if desired. Top with a bread slice, butter-side up. Reduce heat to medium-low. Cook for 3 to 5 minutes, until golden; flip and cook until golden on other side. Repeat to cook remaining sandwiches. Makes 4 sandwiches.

toss-ins for a twist

These yummy sandwiches also taste great made with deli ham or turkey.

White Bean Salad

Sun-dried tomato-infused oil is easier to find than you'd think…just pour it right from the jar of sun-dried tomatoes!

¼ c. extra-virgin olive oil
2 T. sun-dried tomato-infused oil
¼ c. sun-dried tomatoes, chopped
1 T. red wine vinegar
¼ t. salt

¼ t. pepper
2 16-oz. cans cannellini beans, drained and rinsed
⅓ c. red onion, diced
2 cloves garlic, minced
6 leaves basil, thinly sliced
¼ c. grated Romano cheese

Combine olive oil, tomato oil, sun-dried tomatoes, vinegar, salt and pepper in a small bowl; mix well. Place beans in a serving bowl; pour oil mixture over top. Cover; refrigerate for one hour. Toss; sprinkle with onion, garlic, basil and cheese. Serve immediately. Serves 6 to 8.

"I discovered this recipe in my local paper, and it's since become a family favorite."

—Amy

Amy Grounsell
Kansas City, MO

Extra-Cheesy
Grilled Cheese

Toasted Green Tomato Sandwiches

Heat up your skillet to make this hot, buttery favorite. Tomatoes never tasted better...yum!

> *"When my son requested these sandwiches a second time, I realized I'd 'hit the mark!'"*
>
> –Janie

1½ to 2 c. cornmeal
salt, pepper and seasoning salt
  to taste
2 green tomatoes, sliced
  ¼-inch thick

oil or shortening for frying
2 to 3 T. butter, softened
8 slices whole-wheat bread
Optional: basil mayonnaise,
  curly leaf lettuce

Combine cornmeal and seasonings in a large plastic zipping bag. Shake to mix well. Add tomato slices and gently shake to coat. Remove tomatoes from bag, shaking off excess cornmeal mixture. Heat oil or shortening in a large skillet over medium heat; fry tomatoes until golden on both sides. Remove from skillet. Spread butter on one side of each bread slice. Arrange 4 slices, butter-side down, in skillet. Cook over medium heat until toasted. Repeat with remaining bread slices. Spread mayonnaise over untoasted sides of bread, if desired. Top with tomatoes and lettuce, if desired. Top with another slice of bread. Cook sandwiches over medium heat, turning once, until golden on both sides. Makes 4 sandwiches.

Janie Reed
Zanesville, OH

Green Goddess Bacon Salad

Julie Ann Perkins (Anderson, IN)

I grew up loving Green Goddess dressing...my grandmother used it all the time.

7 **eggs**, hard-boiled, peeled and
   sliced
7 to 12 slices **bacon**, crisply cooked
   and crumbled
3 c. **deli roast chicken**, shredded
6 to 8 c. **baby spinach**

1 **red pepper**, chopped
Optional: 1 bunch **green onions**,
   sliced
Green Goddess salad dressing to
   taste

Combine eggs, bacon, chicken, spinach, red pepper and green onions, if desired,
in a large bowl; mix well. Pass salad dressing at the table so guests may add it to
taste. Serves 6.

Taco Salad

Jazz up this yummy salad even more with dollops of sour cream and guacamole.

> "I serve this salad at all of our get-togethers."
>
> —Lisa

1 lb. ground beef, browned
1¼-oz. pkg. taco seasoning mix
1 head lettuce, torn
12 cherry tomatoes, quartered

2 c. shredded Cheddar cheese
6-oz. can sliced olives, drained
8-oz. bottle French dressing
2 7-oz. bags tortilla chips

Prepare ground beef with taco seasoning according to package directions; set aside to cool. Toss lettuce, tomatoes and cheese together; add meat mixture, olives and French dressing. Refrigerate for at least one hour to blend flavors. Before serving, crush tortilla chips and add to the salad; mix well. Serves 6 to 8.

Lisa McMorrow
Phoenix, AZ

Mediterranean Beef Salad

This is one of our favorite warm-weather meals! For a delicious chilled salad, use leftover grilled steak.

1 lb. top sirloin steak,
  1-inch thick
salt and pepper to taste
4 c. romaine lettuce, torn

½ red onion, thinly sliced and
  separated into rings
1 c. cherry tomatoes, halved
½ c. crumbled feta cheese

Broil or grill steak to desired doneness. Sprinkle with salt and pepper to taste. Let steak stand for several minutes; slice thinly. Divide lettuce among 4 plates. Top with sliced steak, onion, tomatoes and cheese. Drizzle with Lemony Dressing. Serves 4.

Lemony Dressing:

¼ c. olive oil
½ t. lemon zest
3 T. lemon juice

1 T. fresh oregano, chopped
2 cloves garlic, minced
salt and pepper to taste

Whisk together all ingredients.

Cheri Maxwell
Gulf Breeze, FL

toss-ins for a twist

This yummy salad is also great with grilled chicken.

keep 'em crisp

Salad greens will stay crisp much longer if they're washed and dried as soon as they're brought home. Wrap them in paper towels to absorb moisture and seal in a plastic zipping bag before tucking them into the crisping drawer of the refrigerator.

Salmon Salad Rena Tauck (Hammond, MT)

This scrumptious salad makes eating right fun! I like to serve my homemade corn fritters with it.

10- to 12-oz. salmon fillet
½ c. lime juice
pepper to taste
4 c. spinach, torn
1 c. sweetened dried cranberries

1 c. crumbled blue cheese
1 c. sugared walnuts
1 tomato, sliced
vinaigrette or blue cheese salad
    dressing to taste

Dip salmon in lime juice on both sides; sprinkle with pepper to taste. Grill over medium-high heat for 4 to 5 minutes per side, until fish flakes easily. Divide spinach, cranberries, cheese, walnuts and tomato slices between 2 plates. Slice salmon in half; place on plates. Drizzle with desired amount of salad dressing. Serves 2.

Panzanella Salad

Enjoy this farm-fresh salad any time of year. If you can't find heirloom tomatoes, large red tomatoes will be just as good.

2 lbs. heirloom tomatoes, diced
¼ c. red onion, minced
2 t. garlic, minced
½ c. olive oil
2 T. lemon juice
2 T. fresh basil, chopped
1 T. fresh tarragon, chopped
1 t. salt
pepper to taste
2 c. arugula leaves
Garnish: grated Parmesan
  cheese

Place tomatoes in a colander to allow liquid to drain. Combine tomatoes, onion, garlic, oil, lemon juice, basil, tarragon, salt and pepper. Top with Homemade Croutons and toss well. Divide tomato mixture among 4 serving plates. Top each serving with arugula; garnish with cheese. Serves 4.

Homemade Croutons:

¼ c. butter
1 T. garlic, minced
6 slices day-old bread, crusts
  trimmed, cubed
salt and pepper to taste
6 T. grated Parmesan cheese

Melt butter in a large skillet over medium heat. Cook until butter foams. Add garlic and cook for 30 seconds to one minute. Add bread cubes and toss to coat. Season with salt and pepper to taste. Place on a lightly greased baking sheet and bake at 375 degrees for 15 minutes, or until lightly golden. Sprinkle with cheese and toss until cheese melts.

Kelly Anderson
Erie, PA

Bountiful Garden Salad

Add grilled chicken to this chock-full salad, if you'd like.

6 c. spinach, torn
1 lb. romaine lettuce, torn
1 stalk celery, chopped
1 red onion, chopped
1 tomato, chopped
½ cucumber, chopped
1 bunch fresh cilantro, chopped
1 clove garlic, finely chopped
½ orange, peeled and sectioned
¾ c. blackberries, raspberries and/or blueberries
¼ c. strawberries, hulled and sliced
¼ c. chopped walnuts or pecans, toasted
Garnish: croutons

Place all ingredients except croutons in a large salad bowl and toss to mix. Drizzle with Raspberry Dressing; garnish with croutons. Serves 6 to 8.

Raspberry Dressing:

¾ c. to 1 c. raspberries, crushed
¼ c. raspberry vinegar
1 T. sugar
2 T. lemon juice
1 c. olive oil
salt and pepper to taste

Combine raspberries, vinegar, sugar and juice; slowly drizzle in oil, whisking constantly to blend. Add salt and pepper to taste.

Joanne Fajack
Youngstown, OH

"Grandma always served this salad when we came to visit. We loved to watch her putting together this big beautiful bowl of pretty colors and delicious fruits. She grew most of the produce in her garden, and the nuts came from the grocery store where Grandpa helped out."

–Joanne

leftover love

If there's leftover chopped salad after dinner, use it for a tasty sandwich filling the next day. Split a pita round, stuff with salad and drizzle with salad dressing...yummy!

Blue Crab Salad

A very flavorful salad that's best served simply…over curly leaf lettuce with your favorite crackers.

6 cloves garlic, minced
2 shallots, minced
¼ c. oil
½ c. sour cream
2-oz. pkg. cream cheese with garlic and fine herbs
1½ t. green hot pepper sauce
¼ t. Worcestershire sauce
1 T. fresh cilantro, chopped
2 T. fresh chives, chopped
juice of 2 limes
1 t. salt
⅛ t. cayenne pepper
1 lb. crabmeat

Sauté garlic and shallots in oil in a skillet over medium-high heat just until translucent; remove from heat. Blend sour cream and cheese in a mixing bowl; stir in hot pepper sauce, Worcestershire sauce, cilantro and chives. Sprinkle with lime juice, salt and cayenne pepper. Stir in garlic mixture and crabmeat, being careful not to break up the crabmeat too finely. Serves 6 to 8.

Kathy Unruh
Fresno, CA

cool server

An ice bowl makes a cool server for seafood salad. Center a small plastic bowl inside a larger one, using masking tape to hold it in place. Arrange citrus slices and sprigs of mint between the bowls, fill with water and freeze until solid. Gently remove both plastic bowls and fill with salad.

Roasted Walnut & Pear Salad

You can serve this wonderful salad for any gathering…from formal dinners to casual family meals. Be sure to use fresh pears for the best flavor.

1 head romaine lettuce, torn
2 c. pears, thinly sliced
2 roma tomatoes, chopped
1 c. walnuts
2 T. butter

¼ c. brown sugar, packed
4-oz. pkg. crumbled blue cheese
8-oz. bottle raspberry white wine salad dressing

toss-ins for a twist

Serve this salad alongside baked chicken or toss in chopped cooked turkey.

Place lettuce in a large serving bowl; place pears on top and add tomatoes. Toast walnuts in butter in a medium skillet until golden; add brown sugar and stir over low heat until walnuts are hardened with glaze. Add walnuts to salad, sprinkle blue cheese over top and toss with desired amount of salad dressing. Serves 6 to 8.

Laurie Johnson
Rosenberg, TX

Fiesta Breakfast Strata, page 178

breakfast anytime

Breakfast foods are so delicious and comforting...so why only serve them in the morning? Everyone will love Nutty Maple Waffles (page 170) and Fiesta Breakfast Strata (page 178). Try Country-Style Breakfast Pizza (page 181) or Ham & Egg Casserole (page 191). With quick prep times and simple ingredients, these dishes are ideal for weeknight dinners!

Grammy's Overnight Pancakes

2 c. long-cooking oats, uncooked
2 c. plus ¼ c. buttermilk,
  divided
½ c. all-purpose flour
½ c. whole-wheat flour
2 t. sugar
1½ t. baking powder
1½ t. baking soda
1 t. salt
2 eggs
2 T. butter, melted and cooled
oil for frying

Combine oats and 2 cups buttermilk in a bowl; cover and refrigerate overnight. To prepare pancakes, stir together flours, sugar, baking powder, baking soda and salt. Set aside. Beat together eggs and butter in a large bowl. Stir into oat mixture. Add flour mixture, stirring well. If batter is too thick, stir in 2 to 4 tablespoons remaining buttermilk. Pour batter by ¼ cupfuls onto a well-greased hot griddle. Cook until bubbles appear on the surface; flip and cook other side until golden. Top with Apple Pancake Syrup. Makes 16 pancakes.

Regina Ferrigno
Gooseberry Patch

"Whenever we visit Grammy, these yummy pancakes are on the breakfast table without fail. Usually they're surrounded by sausage or bacon, scrambled eggs and toast with jam. We can't imagine breakfast any other way!"
—Regina

Apple Pancake Syrup:

My older sister, Teena, often cooked for my siblings and me. She would make this syrup to serve on our breakfast pancakes and waffles…she could really make something from nothing!

6-oz. can frozen sugar-free
  apple juice concentrate,
  thawed
¾ c. water
½ t. lemon juice
1 T. cornstarch
¼ t. cinnamon

Mix all ingredients in a saucepan. Cook over medium heat, stirring frequently, about 15 minutes, until thickened and reduced by half. Serves 4 to 6.

Gail Shepard
Missoula, MT

Scrumptious Blueberry Pancakes

Keep pancakes warm & toasty in a 200-degree oven.

toss-ins for a twist

Try raspberries or blackberries in place of the blueberries for a change of flavor.

1 c. milk
½ c. water
1 c. plus 2 T. whole-wheat flour
½ c. cornmeal
1 t. baking powder

½ t. baking soda
¼ t. salt
1 c. blueberries
2 T. oil, divided
Garnish: jam or syrup

Mix together milk and ½ cup water in a small bowl; set aside. Sift together flour, cornmeal, baking powder, baking soda and salt in a large bowl; mix well. Stir in milk mixture just until combined. Fold in blueberries; let stand 5 minutes. Heat one tablespoon oil in a large skillet over medium heat. Pour ¼ cup batter per pancake into skillet; cook until bubbly on top and edges are slightly dry. Flip and cook other side until golden. Repeat with remaining oil and batter. Serve warm with jam or syrup. Makes one dozen pancakes.

Jo Ann
Gooseberry Patch

Megan's Cinnamon Pancakes

These pancakes fill the house with a sweet cinnamon smell. We love to make them for breakfast on special occasions, especially in chilly weather. We've even enjoyed them for dessert once or twice!

1½ c. all-purpose flour
3½ t. baking powder
1 t. salt
1 T. sugar
1 t. cinnamon
1¼ c. milk

1 egg, beaten
2 T. vanilla extract
3 T. butter, melted and slightly cooled
⅓ c. cinnamon baking chips

Sift together flour, baking powder, salt, sugar and cinnamon into a large bowl. Add milk, egg, vanilla and melted butter; mix until smooth. Fold in cinnamon chips. Lightly grease a griddle or frying pan and heat over medium-high heat. Pour batter onto heated griddle by ¼ cupfuls. Cook until golden on both sides. Serve warm with Cream Cheese Topping. Makes one dozen pancakes.

Cream Cheese Topping:

½ c. cream cheese, softened
¼ c. butter, softened
1 c. powdered sugar

½ t. vanilla extract
¼ t. lemon juice
2 T. milk

Beat together cream cheese and butter until smooth. Add powdered sugar, vanilla, lemon juice and milk; mix until well blended. Serve at room temperature or warmed. May be stored in refrigerator for up to one week.

Megan Dulgarian
Moore, OK

Nutty Maple Waffles
Vickie (Gooseberry Patch)

1½ c. all-purpose flour
2 T. sugar
1 t. baking powder
¼ t. salt
2 eggs, separated

12-oz. can evaporated milk
3 T. oil
½ t. maple extract
½ c. pecans, finely chopped

Combine flour, sugar, baking powder and salt in a medium bowl; mix well and set aside. Combine egg yolks, evaporated milk, oil and maple extract in a large bowl; blend well. Gradually add flour mixture, beating well after each addition; set aside. Beat egg whites in a small bowl with an electric mixer at high speed until stiff peaks form; fold into batter. For each waffle, pour ½ cup batter onto a preheated, greased waffle iron; sprinkle with one tablespoon nuts. Cook according to manufacturer's instructions. Serves 8.

Strawberry French Toast

Such a treat...perfect for a weekend brunch.

3 **eggs**, beaten
¾ c. **half-and-half**
1 T. **strawberry jam**
8 thick slices **French bread**,
  halved diagonally

2 to 3 T. **butter**
Garnish: sliced **strawberries**,
  powdered sugar

Whisk together eggs, half-and-half and jam in a shallow bowl. Dip bread into mixture. Melt butter in a skillet over medium heat; cook bread on both sides until golden. Serve toast topped with a large dollop of Strawberry Butter, sliced strawberries and a dusting of powdered sugar. Serves 3 to 4.

Strawberry Butter:

⅓ c. **strawberry jam**

¼ c. **butter**, softened

Beat jam and butter with an electric mixer at low speed until well blended. Serve at room temperature.

Rosemary Zins
Alexandria, MN

supper in a snap

Make the strawberry butter ahead of time and serve with microwavable sausage patties. It's so easy!

Make-Ahead Pumpkin Pie French Toast

This casserole is great for a weeknight supper! Make and refrigerate it in the morning to serve around dinnertime.

> "I combined several different French toast recipes to suit my family's tastes. They love anything with pumpkin, so the pumpkin pie spice was a must. It's a great Sunday morning breakfast, or it can bake while you get ready for church. It's also super-easy for husbands to whip up, so Mom can sleep in just a bit on Saturday morning!"
>
> –Jennifer

1 loaf French, Italian, challah or Hawaiian bread, cut into 1-inch slices
3 eggs, beaten
½ c. egg substitute
1 c. half-and-half
1½ c. milk
¼ t. salt
1 t. vanilla extract
1 T. pumpkin pie spice
½ c. brown sugar, packed
1 to 2 T. butter, sliced

Arrange bread slices in the bottom of a greased 13"x9" baking pan. Whisk together eggs, egg substitute, half-and-half, milk, salt, vanilla and spice. Stir in brown sugar; pour mixture over bread slices. Refrigerate, covered, overnight. Dot top with butter and bake, uncovered, at 350 degrees for 40 to 45 minutes. Serves 8.

Jennifer Yandle
Indian Trail, NC

"eggseptional" tip

When breaking eggs, if part of a broken eggshell makes its way into the bowl, just dip in a clean eggshell half. The broken bit will grab onto it like a magnet!

Monte Christian Sandwiches

While camping with our son, Christian, we asked him what he wanted for breakfast the next day. He thought about the breakfast items we had brought with us and came up with these sandwiches. They tasted so good that I told him I would send the recipe to Gooseberry Patch, and here it is!

1 T. butter, divided
4 eggs, divided
¼ c. milk
4 slices bread
Optional: 2 slices favorite
   cheese

2 pork sausage breakfast
   patties, browned and drained
Optional: maple syrup

Melt ½ tablespoon butter in a skillet over medium heat. Whisk 2 eggs with milk in a shallow bowl. Dip bread slices into egg mixture; cook in skillet until golden on both sides. Set aside; keep warm. Add remaining butter to skillet; break remaining eggs into skillet and cook over easy with yolks set. Top eggs with cheese, if desired, and cover skillet until cheese melts. To assemble, place one slice bread on a plate, top with an egg, a sausage patty and a second slice of bread. Repeat to make a second sandwich. Slice in half and eat as a sandwich or drizzle with syrup and eat with a knife and fork. Makes 2 sandwiches.

Michele Edmonds
Red Hook, NY

toss-ins for a twist

Try Canadian bacon or deli ham in place of the sausage, if you'd like.

retro fun

Add a dash of whimsy to the table...serve cream or pancake syrup in a vintage can-shaped creamer.

Breakfast Apple Sandwiches

16.3-oz. tube refrigerated
  jumbo biscuits
8-oz. pkg. shredded Cheddar
  cheese, divided
2 apples, cored and sliced into
  16 rings

2 T. cinnamon
¼ c. brown sugar, packed
¼ c. butter, melted

Split biscuits. Lay each biscuit half on an ungreased baking sheet.
Sprinkle about 2 tablespoons of cheese on each biscuit. Top with an apple
ring. Mix together cinnamon and brown sugar in a bowl. Spoon some
cinnamon-sugar on top of each apple ring. Top with a small amount of
butter. Bake, uncovered, at 400 degrees for 15 to 20 minutes, until golden.
Makes 16 sandwiches.

Sarah Allen
Longview, TX

"This is one of my
son's favorite recipes.
I've been making them
for him since he was
about four years old...
now he's 21! We like
to use crisp Granny
Smith apples."
—Sarah

Blueberry-Sausage Breakfast Cake

An all-in-one breakfast that's extra special.

2 c. all-purpose flour
1 t. baking powder
½ t. baking soda
½ c. butter
¾ c. sugar
¼ c. brown sugar, packed
8-oz. container sour cream
2 eggs
1 lb. ground pork breakfast
    sausage, browned and
    drained
1 c. blueberries
½ c. chopped pecans

Mix flour, baking powder and baking soda in a bowl; set aside. Beat butter until fluffy in a large bowl with an electric mixer at medium speed. Add sugars and sour cream; beat until combined. Add eggs, one at a time, beating just until combined. Add butter mixture to flour mixture. Fold in sausage and berries. Pour batter into an ungreased 13"x9" baking pan. Spread evenly in pan; sprinkle pecans on top. Bake, uncovered, at 350 degrees for 35 to 40 minutes, until a toothpick comes out clean. Cool on a wire rack; cut into squares. Serve with warm Blueberry Sauce. Serves 15.

Blueberry Sauce:

½ c. sugar
2 T. cornstarch
½ c. water
2 c. blueberries
½ c. lemon juice

Combine sugar and cornstarch in a medium saucepan; add ½ cup water and berries. Cook and stir over medium heat until thickened and bubbly. Cook and stir 2 more minutes. Stir in lemon juice; cool slightly before pouring over cake.

Sarah Hoech
Bismark, ND

Smith Family Breakfast Bake

12-oz. tube refrigerated
  biscuits, baked and torn
1 lb. ground pork breakfast
  sausage, browned and drained
8 eggs, beaten
2 c. milk
1 sprig fresh rosemary, chopped

1 t. Italian seasoning
1 t. dried basil
1 t. dried oregano
1 t. dried thyme
salt and pepper to taste
8-oz. pkg. shredded Cheddar
  cheese

"I created this recipe to duplicate one that I tasted and loved. Now my kids and husband love it too!"

—Cherylann

Arrange torn biscuits in a lightly greased 13"x9" baking pan. Top with sausage; set aside. Blend eggs and milk with seasonings in a large bowl. Pour over sausage; sprinkle with cheese. Bake, uncovered, at 350 degrees for 30 minutes, or until golden. Serves 12.

Cherylann Smith
Efland, NC

Fiesta Breakfast Strata

I created this recipe because I love Mexican food. Homemade salsa is easier than you'd think, and every time I make this, I'm asked to share the recipe.

1 lb. ground beef
8-oz. can tomato sauce
2 t. chili powder
½ t. garlic powder
salt and pepper to taste
5 10-inch flour tortillas
16-oz. can refried beans, divided

8-oz. pkg. shredded sharp
   Cheddar cheese, divided
1 red pepper, diced
2 tomatoes, diced
5 green onions, chopped
Optional: salsa, sour cream

Brown beef in a skillet; drain. Add tomato sauce and seasonings. Simmer until mixture thickens; set aside. Line the bottom of a 9" springform pan with aluminum foil. Place one tortilla in the bottom of the pan. Spread half the refried beans on tortilla and top with half the ground beef mixture. Top with ⅓ of the cheese. Layer a second tortilla over cheese; sprinkle with half each red pepper, tomatoes and onions. Add a third tortilla and spread with remaining refried beans, beef mixture and ⅓ cheese. Layer on a fourth tortilla and top with remaining red pepper and tomatoes. Add last tortilla and cover with remaining cheese and onions. Bake, uncovered, at 350 degrees for one hour, or until heated through. Serve with salsa and sour cream, if desired. Serves 6 to 8.

Salsa:

1 orange, red or yellow
   pepper, diced
1 jalapeño pepper, seeded
   and diced
½ red onion, diced

1 tomato, diced
½ c. fresh cilantro, chopped
1 T. lemon juice
salt and pepper to taste

Combine all ingredients in a serving bowl or container; refrigerate for one hour.

supper in a snap

Homemade fresh salsa is so easy to prepare, but to save time pick up some in the deli section, if you'd like.

Yvette Nelson
British Columbia, Canada

Flaky Ham + Egg Bake

Serve this breakfast casserole with some fresh fruit to complete the meal.

8-oz. tube refrigerated crescent
   rolls
6 eggs, beaten
½ c. mushrooms, chopped

1 c. cooked ham, chopped
1½ c. shredded Cheddar
   cheese

"I made this for my kids when they were little. They're all grown up now, but when they come to visit, it's always requested!"
—Donna

   Unroll crescents and place in a single layer in a lightly greased 9" pie plate; press seams together. Pour eggs over top. Sprinkle with mushrooms, ham and cheese. Bake, uncovered, at 375 degrees for 15 to 18 minutes, until golden. Serves 6.

Donna Healy
Mountain Home, ID

Country-Style Breakfast Pizza

A surefire breakfast hit…you'll get requests for this recipe!

13.8-oz. tube refrigerated pizza crust dough
Optional: garlic salt
24-oz. pkg. refrigerated mashed potatoes
10 eggs, beaten
Optional: chopped vegetables, cooked ham or sausage
8-oz. pkg. shredded Colby Jack cheese
4-oz. pkg. crumbled bacon pieces

Spread pizza crust dough in a pizza pan; sprinkle with garlic salt, if desired, and set aside. Place mashed potatoes in a microwave-safe bowl; microwave on high setting for about 5 minutes, until heated through. Spread potatoes over dough. Scramble eggs as desired, adding vegetables, ham or sausage, if desired. Spread scrambled eggs evenly over potatoes. Sprinkle with cheese; top with bacon. Bake at 350 degrees for 30 minutes, or until cheese is melted and bubbly. Serves 8.

Jackie Balla
Walbridge, OH

supper in a snap

This pizza is a family favorite. Prepare all the toppings in advance, and let the little ones pile on their favorite toppings!

jewel-like juice

Serve breakfast juices in glasses with a bit of sparkle. Run a lemon wedge around the rims of glasses and then dip the rims in superfine sugar. Garnish each with a sprig of fresh mint.

Mini Quiches

supper in a snap

Instead of rolling out pastry for 24 mini quiches, use this recipe to make one large quiche, too! Just add an egg, double all other ingredients, pour into a pie crust and bake until set.

2 9-inch refrigerated pie crusts, unbaked
2 eggs
½ c. milk
¾ c. zucchini, chopped
½ c. mushrooms, chopped

½ c. shredded Cheddar cheese
¼ c. cooked ham, diced
¼ c. green onions, sliced
1 clove garlic, minced
salt and pepper to taste

Roll out each pie crust into a 12"x12" square on a lightly floured surface; using a glass, cut each square into 12 circles. Press into greased mini muffin pans; set aside. Whisk together eggs and milk in a bowl; stir in remaining ingredients. Spoon about one tablespoon of filling into each muffin cup; bake at 375 degrees for 15 to 18 minutes, until puffed and golden. Cool in pan for 2 to 3 minutes; carefully remove and serve warm. Makes 2 dozen mini quiches.

Kerrie Miller
Kerman, CA

Beef + Cheddar Quiche

Dianne Young (South Jordan, UT)

So yummy topped with sour cream or even salsa!

3 eggs, beaten
1 c. whipping cream
1 c. shredded Cheddar cheese

1 c. ground beef, browned
9-inch pie crust

Mix eggs, cream, cheese and beef together; spread into pie crust. Bake, uncovered, at 450 degrees for 15 minutes; lower oven temperature to 350 degrees and bake 15 more minutes. Serves 8.

Crab, Corn & Pepper Frittata

Stacie Avner (Delaware, OH)

6 eggs, beaten
¼ c. milk
⅓ c. mayonnaise
2 T. green onions, chopped
2 T. red pepper, chopped
⅓ c. corn

salt and pepper to taste
1 c. crabmeat
1 c. shredded Monterey Jack
  cheese
Optional: additional chopped green
  onions

Whisk together eggs, milk, mayonnaise, onions, red pepper, corn, salt and pepper in a large bowl. Gently stir in crabmeat. Pour into a greased 10" pie plate. Bake, uncovered, at 350 degrees for 15 to 20 minutes. Sprinkle with cheese and bake for 5 more minutes, or until cheese melts. Garnish with green onions, if desired. Serves 4 to 6.

Spanish Omelet

Serve this omelet in hearty wedges with a chunky tomato & onion salad…delicious!

¼ c. olive oil, divided
1 to 2 potatoes, peeled and diced
1 onion, sliced
1 red pepper, diced
1 green pepper, diced
1 zucchini, coarsely chopped

⅓ to ½ c. frozen peas
¼ lb. smoked chorizo or Kielbasa sausage, diced
5 eggs, lightly beaten
salt and pepper to taste
½ c. shredded Cheddar cheese

Heat 2 tablespoons oil in an oven-proof skillet over high heat. Add potatoes and onion; toss to coat well. Reduce heat to medium-low. Cover and cook for 15 minutes, stirring occasionally. Add peppers, zucchini, peas and sausage; mix well. Cover and cook 5 to 8 more minutes, until vegetables start to soften. Combine eggs, salt and pepper in a large bowl. Remove skillet from heat; slowly pour vegetable mixture into bowl with eggs. Add remaining oil to skillet and place over medium-high heat. Pour egg and vegetable mixture into skillet; cook for one minute. Reduce heat to low; cook, uncovered, for 15 to 20 minutes. Sprinkle omelet with cheese; place under broiler for 3 to 5 minutes, until golden and bubbly. Cut into wedges to serve. Serves 4.

"This is a great big thick cake of an omelet packed with vegetables and cheese. It can be served warm as a main course, and it tastes just as good cold. You can even take it on a picnic."

–Elaine

Elaine Day
Essex, England

California Omelet

"Enjoy an unhurried breakfast with your family...at dinnertime! An omelet or frittata is perfect. Just add a basket of muffins, fresh fruit and a steamy pot of tea."

—Christina

1 T. oil
3 to 4 eggs
¼ c. milk
salt and pepper to taste

1 avocado, sliced
2 to 3 green onions, diced
½ c. shredded Monterey Jack cheese

Heat oil in a skillet over medium-low heat. Whisk together eggs, milk, salt and pepper in a bowl; pour into skillet. Cook until eggs are lightly golden on bottom and partially set on top. Sprinkle with remaining ingredients; carefully fold omelet in half so that toppings are covered. Reduce heat to medium-low and cook, uncovered, about 10 minutes. Serves 2.

Christina Mendoza
Alamogordo, NM

Farmers' Market Omelet

Toss in your favorite farm-fresh veggies!

1 t. olive oil
2 T. bacon, diced
2 T. onion, chopped
2 T. zucchini, diced

5 cherry tomatoes, quartered
¼ t. fresh thyme, minced
3 eggs, beaten
¼ c. fontina cheese, shredded

Heat oil in a skillet over medium-high heat. Add bacon and onion; cook and stir until bacon is crisp and onion is tender. Add zucchini, tomatoes and thyme. Allow to cook until zucchini is soft and juice from tomatoes has slightly evaporated. Lower heat to medium and add eggs, stirring eggs to cook evenly. Continue to cook, lifting edges to allow uncooked egg to flow underneath. When eggs are almost fully cooked, sprinkle cheese over top and fold over. Serves one.

Vickie
Gooseberry Patch

"I love visiting the farmers' market bright & early on Saturday mornings...a terrific way to begin the day!"
—Vickie

Kathy's Bacon Popovers

Mmm...bacon! An easy tote-along breakfast to enjoy on the go.

2 eggs
1 c. milk
1 T. oil
1 c. all-purpose flour

½ t. salt
3 slices bacon, crisply cooked
  and crumbled

Whisk together eggs, milk and oil. Beat in flour and salt just until smooth. Fill 12 greased and floured muffin cups ⅔ full. Sprinkle bacon evenly over batter. Bake at 400 degrees for 25 to 30 minutes, until puffed and golden. Serve warm. Makes one dozen.

Kathy Grashoff
Fort Wayne, IN

Country-Style Supper Skillet

Eggs, fresh tomatoes, bacon and potatoes make up this hearty dish...you'll serve it again and again.

½ lb. bacon, chopped
3 c. potatoes, peeled, cooked
  and diced
1 c. tomato, chopped
½ c. onion, chopped
½ c. green pepper, chopped

1 t. garlic, chopped
½ t. salt
¼ t. pepper
1½ c. shredded sharp Cheddar
  cheese
8 eggs

Cook bacon over medium heat in a large deep skillet until crisp; partially drain drippings, reserving some in skillet. Add vegetables, garlic, salt and pepper to skillet; sauté in pan drippings 5 minutes, or until tender. Sprinkle with cheese. Make 8 wells for eggs; crack eggs into wells about 2 inches apart. Reduce heat; cover and cook eggs over medium heat for 10 to 12 minutes, until eggs reach desired degree of doneness. Serves 4 to 6.

Rita Morgan
Pueblo, CO

season's best

Visit a nearby farmers' market for just-harvested fruits & vegetables, eggs, baked goods, jams & jellies...perfect for farm-fresh breakfast!

10-Gallon Hash

This hearty meal will satisfy the whole family.

1½ lbs. ground beef, browned
2 to 3 c. onions, sliced
1 green pepper, thinly sliced
⅛ t. garlic powder
2 t. chili powder

salt and pepper to taste
14½-oz. can stewed tomatoes
1 c. water
¾ c. instant rice, uncooked

toss-ins for a twist

Top with a fried egg for a spicy breakfast treat.

Combine all ingredients except rice in a large skillet; bring to a boil, stirring often. Add rice; cover and remove from heat. Let stand about 5 minutes, until rice is tender. Serves 4.

Wendy Lee Paffenroth
Pine Island, NY

Smoked Sausage Breakfast Burritos

1 to 2 T. olive oil
1 onion, diced
14-oz. smoked pork sausage
   ring, diced
1 tomato, diced

6 eggs, beaten
salt and pepper to taste
4 to 6 flour or corn tortillas
salsa

Heat oil in a large skillet over medium-high heat. Add onion; sauté until tender. Add sausage; cook and stir until browned. Add tomato and cook until heated through. Add eggs; scramble as desired. Season with salt and pepper to taste. Wrap tortillas in a damp tea towel; microwave 30 seconds, or until heated. To serve, spoon egg mixture into tortillas; top with salsa and roll up. Serves 4 to 6.

Sherry Pate
Conley, GA

Garden Tomato Rarebit

Spoon this cheesy dish over slices of country-style bread...yummy all day!

2 T. butter
2 T. all-purpose flour
1 c. light cream, warmed
⅛ t. baking soda
½ c. tomatoes, finely chopped
2 c. shredded Cheddar cheese

2 eggs, lightly beaten
1 t. dry mustard
fresh basil to taste, chopped
cayenne pepper to taste
salt and pepper to taste
6 slices bread, toasted

Melt butter in a saucepan over medium heat. Stir in flour; cook and stir 2 to 3 minutes. Slowly pour in cream; cook and stir until mixture thickens. Combine baking soda and tomatoes in a small bowl, stirring to mix. Add tomato mixture to saucepan; stir in cheese, eggs, mustard, basil, cayenne pepper, salt and pepper. Reduce heat to low; cook and stir until cheese melts. Do not boil. To serve, spoon mixture over slices of toast. Serves 6.

Marcia Shaffer
Conneaut Lake, PA

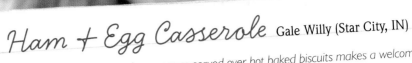

Ham + Egg Casserole Gale Willy (Star City, IN)

Cubed ham in a creamy cheese sauce served over hot baked biscuits makes a welcoming meal any time of day.

½ t. onion powder
5 eggs, hard-boiled and chopped
10¾-oz. can cream of chicken
   soup
¼ c. milk

2 c. shredded Cheddar cheese
1 c. cooked ham, cubed
12-oz. tube refrigerated biscuits,
   baked

Combine onion powder, eggs, soup, milk and cheese in a medium bowl; blend well. Spoon mixture in a greased 8"x8" baking dish. Spread ham evenly over top. Bake, uncovered, at 350 degrees for 25 minutes. Serve over biscuits. Serves 4 to 6.

Maple Ham & Egg Cups

Ham and eggs make such a great breakfast or brunch...the kids will love the novelty too.

1 T. butter, melted
6 slices deli ham
1 T. maple syrup
1 t. butter, cut into 6 pieces

6 eggs
salt and pepper to taste
English muffins, toast or
  biscuits

Brush muffin cups in pans with melted butter; line each cup with a slice of ham. Pour ½ teaspoon maple syrup over each ham slice; top with one pat of butter. Crack one egg into each ham cup; season with salt and pepper to taste. Bake at 400 degrees for 20 minutes, or until eggs are set. Remove muffin cups from oven; use a spoon or gently twist each serving to loosen. Serve on English muffins, toast or split biscuits. Serves 6.

Staci Meyers
Montezuma, GA

Creamy Ambrosia Salad

On busy mornings, I love having a big bowl of this sweet, healthy fruit salad ready for my family's breakfast. It only requires a handful of ingredients and takes just minutes to put together.

½ c. mayonnaise
1 c. plain or vanilla yogurt
30-oz. can fruit cocktail,
  drained
20-oz. can pineapple chunks,
  drained

5-oz. pkg. sweetened flaked
  coconut
½ c. raisins
½ c. chopped walnuts

Blend mayonnaise and yogurt in a large bowl. Stir in remaining ingredients. Cover and refrigerate for 2 hours, or until thoroughly chilled. Serves 8 to 10.

Amber Carlson
Irvine, CA

Speedy Huevos Rancheros

I like to serve these eggs with fresh diced avocado for a deliciously different breakfast!

6 eggs, beaten
¼ c. water
1 T. butter
1 c. mild salsa
15-oz. can black beans, drained
  and rinsed

¾ c. shredded Mexican-blend
  cheese
8 corn tortillas, warmed
Garnish: fresh cilantro, chopped

Whisk eggs and ¼ cup water together in a bowl. Melt butter in a skillet over medium heat. Add egg mixture; cook for one to 1½ minutes, until eggs just begin to set, stirring constantly. Spoon salsa over eggs; top with beans and cheese. Cover; cook 2 to 3 more minutes, until cheese melts and beans are heated through. Do not stir. Garnish with cilantro; serve with tortillas. Serves 4.

Jill Ross
Pickerington, OH

Poached Pesto Eggs

I'm always looking for new ideas for my husband's breakfast. I thought pesto and eggs would be a good combination. He loved it!

2 eggs
2 to 3 T. basil pesto sauce

2 slices bread, toasted
Garnish: chopped fresh parsley

Add 2 inches water to a skillet. Bring to a simmer over high heat. Break eggs one at a time into a cup and slide into simmering water. Cook eggs for 3 to 5 minutes, until desired doneness. Spread pesto over toast slices. Top each slice with an egg using a slotted spoon. Sprinkle with parsley. Serves one to 2.

Terri Carr
Lewes, DE

toss-ins for a twist

Add even more flavor to this delicious meal by placing tomato slices over the toast slices and adding some herbs to the bacon. Rosemary or thyme are great!

Mountaintop Bacon

My aunt in West Virginia shared this recipe with me …it's a family favorite!

½ c. all-purpose flour
¼ c. brown sugar, packed

1 t. pepper
1 lb. thickly sliced bacon

Mix flour, sugar and pepper together; sprinkle on bacon slices. Place bacon on a greased baking sheet; bake at 400 degrees for 10 to 15 minutes, until browned and crisp. Serves 4 to 6.

Wendy Jacobs
Idaho Falls, ID

Heat + Hold Scrambled Eggs

Serve with a stack of buttered toast and a platter of sizzling sausage…yum!

1 doz. eggs, beaten	2 T. all-purpose flour
1⅓ c. milk	1 T. pimento, chopped
1 t. salt	1 T. fresh parsley, chopped
⅛ t. pepper	¼ c. butter

Combine all ingredients except butter in a large bowl. Whisk until smooth; set aside. Melt butter in a large skillet over low heat; pour egg mixture into skillet. Cook and stir until desired doneness. Can hold for up to one hour in a chafing dish or an electric skillet set at 200 degrees. Serves 6.

Judy Collins
Nashville, TN

supper in a snap

This meal is ready to go when you are. Make the sausage patties ahead and when you can snag a little bit of free time in the afternoon, make the eggs. They will hold for about an hour.

Farmhouse Sausage Patties

Adding your own special ingredients to plain sausage really makes it taste terrific. It's great crumbled for sausage gravy or shaped into patties with eggs and toast for a real country breakfast.

1 lb. ground pork	1 t. salt
1 t. ground cumin	½ t. pepper
½ t. dried thyme	Optional: ⅛ t. cayenne pepper
½ t. dried sage	

Combine pork, cumin, thyme, sage, salt, pepper and cayenne pepper, if desired; mix well. Cover and refrigerate overnight to allow flavors to blend. Form into six 3-inch or twelve 1½-inch patties. Place in a lightly greased skillet over medium heat and brown both sides. Serves 6.

Scrambled Eggs + Lox

Jackie Smulski (Lyons, IL)

These eggs are sure to please everyone…excellent with toasted English muffins or bagels.

6 eggs, beaten
1 T. fresh dill, minced
1 T. fresh chives, minced
1 T. green onion, minced

pepper to taste
2 T. butter
4-oz. pkg. smoked salmon, diced

Whisk together eggs, herbs, onion and pepper. Melt butter in a large skillet over medium heat. Add egg mixture and stir gently with a fork or spatula until eggs begin to set. Stir in salmon and continue cooking until desired doneness. Serves 6.

Sausage + Cheddar Grits

4 c. water
1 t. salt
1 c. quick-cooking grits,
  uncooked
4 eggs, beaten
1 lb. ground pork sausage,
  browned and drained

1½ c. shredded Cheddar
  cheese, divided
1 c. milk
¼ c. butter

Bring water and salt to a boil in a large saucepan over medium heat. Stir in grits; cook for 4 to 5 minutes. Remove from heat. Stir a small amount of hot grits mixture into eggs; add egg mixture to saucepan and stir to mix. Add sausage, one cup cheese, milk and butter; blend together well. Pour into a greased 13"x9" baking pan. Sprinkle with remaining cheese. Bake, uncovered, at 350 degrees for one hour, or until cheese is golden. If cheese is golden early, cover with aluminum foil. Let cool for 10 minutes before serving. Serves 6 to 8.

Sharon Brown
Orange Park, FL

Mile-High Buttermilk Biscuits

2 c. all-purpose flour
1 T. baking powder
1 t. salt

½ c. shortening, chilled
⅔ to ¾ c. buttermilk
¼ c. butter, melted

Mix together flour, baking powder and salt. Cut in shortening until mixture is crumbly. Stir in buttermilk until incorporated and dough leaves sides of bowl. Dough will be sticky. Knead dough 3 to 4 times on a lightly floured surface. Roll out to ½-inch thickness, about 2 to 4 passes with a rolling pin. Cut dough with a biscuit cutter, pressing straight down with cutter. Place biscuits on a parchment paper-lined baking sheet. Bake at 500 degrees for 8 to 10 minutes. Brush tops of warm biscuits with melted butter. Makes about one dozen.

Staci Meyers
Montezuma, GA

Lemony Orzo Salad,
page 219

super simple sides

Side dishes can make a meal memorable...and these recipes will be your go-to guide. Try Creamy Country Corn (page 205) and Anna Rae's Baby Limas (page 213) with a rotisserie chicken you picked up on the way home. Or serve Country-Time Green Beans (page 209) and Herbed Mashed Potatoes (page 215) with your family's favorite pot roast, a recipe you know by heart. Cordie's Spicy Baked Beans (page 214) and Confetti Coleslaw (page 211) will go great with the pork barbecue you picked up from your favorite barbecue joint or have left over from a weekend picnic.

Stuffed Eggplant Boats

Eggplants stay fresh for just a few days, so it's best to keep them stored, unwrapped, in the crisper of the refrigerator.

2 eggplants, peeled and halved lengthwise

1 t. salt

non-stick vegetable spray

2 potatoes, peeled and chopped

¼ c. olive oil, divided

1 c. onion, diced

1 red pepper, diced

2 cloves garlic, minced

salt and pepper to taste

8-oz. pkg. shredded mozzarella cheese

1 c. dry bread crumbs

Scoop out the middles of eggplant halves to form boats. Lightly salt boats; spray with non-stick vegetable spray on all sides. Set aside on a greased baking sheet. Cook potatoes in 3 tablespoons olive oil in a skillet until golden. Remove with a slotted spoon to a separate plate. Add onion, red pepper and garlic to skillet. Cook until onion is translucent and pepper is tender. Return potatoes to pan; sprinkle with salt and pepper to taste. Fill eggplant boats with mixture. Top with cheese and bread crumbs; drizzle with remaining oil. Bake at 350 degrees for 30 minutes, or until tender. Serve immediately. Serves 4.

Michelle Papp
Rutherford, NJ

Minted Baby Carrots

½ lb. baby carrots

2 T. butter

salt and pepper to taste

1 T. lemon zest, minced

1 T. brown sugar, packed

2 t. fresh mint, minced

Cook carrots in boiling water in a stockpot for 5 minutes. Remove from heat and drain. Melt butter in a skillet over medium-high heat. Stir in carrots; cook until crisp-tender. Season with salt and pepper to taste. Combine remaining ingredients and sprinkle over individual servings. Serves 4.

Tori Willis
Champaign, IL

Marinated Tomatoes   Mary Baker (Fountain, NC)

In-season, vine-ripened tomatoes are extra tasty when paired with fresh herbs in this dish.

1 clove garlic, minced
1 t. fresh thyme, chopped
¼ c. green onions, chopped
¼ c. fresh parsley, minced
1 t. salt

¼ t. pepper
6 tomatoes, thickly sliced
¼ t. balsamic vinegar
⅓ c. oil

Combine garlic, thyme, green onions, parsley, salt and pepper; sprinkle over tomatoes. Set aside. Stir together vinegar and oil; pour over tomatoes. Cover and refrigerate for at least 2 hours. Mix gently before serving. Serves 10.

Grilled Market Veggies

I just love to take my roomy market basket to the farmers' market. It's great fun to bring home a bushel of veggies, herbs and new recipes to try!

2 to 3 zucchini, sliced ¾-inch thick
2 to 3 yellow squash, sliced ¾-inch thick
1 to 2 baby eggplant, sliced ¾-inch thick
1 sweet onion, sliced ¾-inch thick
2 tomatoes, sliced 1-inch thick

½ c. balsamic vinegar
1½ c. olive oil
2 cloves garlic, minced
1 T. sugar
1 T. fresh rosemary, chopped
1 T. fresh oregano, chopped
1 T. fresh basil, chopped
1 T. fresh parsley, chopped
salt and pepper to taste

Combine vegetables in a large bowl. Whisk together remaining ingredients and pour over vegetables. Toss to coat. Marinate for 30 minutes to one hour. Remove vegetables from marinade with a slotted spoon. Arrange on a grill over medium heat. Grill for 2 to 5 minutes on each side, until tender, basting often with marinade. Serves 4 to 6.

Regina Wickline
Pebble Beach, CA

slow-cooker hearty vegetable soup

Make a big pot of vegetable soup using vegetables left over from dinner. Keep a container in the freezer just for saving leftover veggies. When you have enough, thaw and place in a slow cooker. Add a can of tomato sauce, water to cover and favorite seasonings to taste. Cover and cook on low all day…delicious and economical!

Creamy Country Corn

6 green onions, chopped
3 T. butter
16-oz. pkg. frozen corn, thawed
2 t. cornstarch
½ c. half-and-half

¼ c. water
½ t. salt
¼ to ½ t. pepper
1 c. cherry tomatoes, halved

Sauté onions in butter in a skillet over medium heat for 2 to 3 minutes, until tender. Stir in corn; cover and cook for 4 to 5 minutes, until heated through. Combine cornstarch, half-and-half, ¼ cup water, salt and pepper in a small bowl; whisk until smooth. Stir into corn mixture. Bring to a boil. Cook, uncovered, for 2 minutes, or until thickened. Stir in tomatoes. Serves 6.

Sharon Demers
Dolores, CO

supper in a snap

This easy recipe makes a tasty accompaniment for grilled meat and a crisp green tossed salad.

Roasted Corn with Rosemary Butter

The next time you fire up the grill, make room for this corn on the cob. Nothing could be better than fresh sweet corn roasted in the husk. Peak season for corn is May through September…enjoy its abundance!

6 ears yellow or white sweet corn, in husks

¼ c. butter, softened
1 t. fresh rosemary, chopped

Pull back corn husks, leaving them attached. Remove and discard silks. Combine butter and rosemary in a small bowl; brush over corn. Pull husks over corn and grill corn over medium-high heat (350 to 400 degrees) for about 15 minutes, turning occasionally. Serves 6.

Zucchini Fritters

Zucchini Fritters

Here's a tasty way to get your family to eat their vegetables…and use the surplus zucchini from your garden!

2 zucchini, grated (about 3½ c.)
1 egg
⅔ c. shredded Cheddar cheese
⅔ c. round buttery crackers, crumbled

Optional: ½ t. seasoned salt
2 T. oil

Combine zucchini, egg, cheese, crackers and, if desired, salt in a large bowl. If mixture seems wet, add extra crackers; shape mixture into patties. Heat oil in a skillet; fry patties for 3 minutes on each side, or until golden. Serves 4.

Melissa Hart
Middleville, MI

toss-ins for a twist

These are also great made with yellow squash.

Quick Squash Sauté

2 T. olive oil
1 onion, sliced
4 zucchini and/or yellow squash, halved lengthwise and sliced

1 t. dried oregano
1 t. garlic powder
salt and pepper to taste

Heat olive oil in a large skillet over medium-high heat. Add onion; sauté for about one minute. Add remaining ingredients. Reduce heat to medium and cook for 10 more minutes, or until vegetables are crisp-tender. Serves 4 to 6.

Jo Ann
Gooseberry Patch

"My whole family likes this quick-to-fix side. It's especially tasty with squash from the farmers' market, but we enjoy it year 'round with squash from the supermarket."

—Jo Ann

Brussels Sprouts Medley

The salad dressing is optional, and this dish is actually good without it.

"I never liked the 'mini cabbages' my mother boiled for our holiday meals. That is, until I tried them done in this creative way! Now I go back for seconds."

—Wendy

6 to 8 thick slices smoky bacon, sliced into 1-inch pieces
1 sweet onion, diced
3 to 4 c. Brussels sprouts, trimmed
½ c. crumbled feta cheese
salt and pepper to taste
Optional: ¼ c. zesty Italian salad dressing

Cook bacon in a skillet over medium heat until crisp. Remove bacon to a plate, reserving drippings in skillet. Sauté onion in drippings. Separate Brussels sprouts into individual leaves, cutting the centers if too tight. Add leaves to skillet. Reduce heat to low; cover and steam until wilted. Return bacon to skillet; stir in cheese, salt and pepper. Top with dressing, if desired. Serve warm. Serves 4 to 6.

Wendy Siladji
Alberta, Canada

Onion Rings

Crispy and delicious with just a hint of sweetness!

supper in a snap

While the onions are soaking for 30 minutes, put your burgers on the grill to cook and heat the frying oil. The burgers will be done and standing while you fry the onion rings.

3 sweet onions, thickly sliced and separated into rings
1½ t. baking powder
1 c. all-purpose flour
1 t. salt
1 egg
⅔ c. water
½ T. lemon juice
1 T. butter, melted
oil for deep-frying

Soak onion rings in ice water for ½ hour; pat dry with paper towels and set aside. Sift baking powder, flour and salt together; set aside. Combine egg, ⅔ cup water and lemon juice; beat well. Stir into flour mixture just until blended; add butter. Heat oil in a deep fryer to 375 degrees. Dip onion rings into batter; drop into hot oil and fry 2 minutes on each side. Drain. Serves 6.

Jo Ann
Gooseberry Patch

Fried Pecan Okra

You can use a 16-ounce package of frozen cut okra, thawed, if you'd rather have bite-size pieces.

1 c. pecans
1½ c. biscuit baking mix
1 t. salt
½ t. pepper

2 10-oz. pkgs. frozen whole okra, thawed
peanut oil

Place pecans in an even layer in a shallow pan. Bake at 350 degrees for 10 minutes, or until lightly toasted, stirring occasionally. Process pecans, baking mix, and salt and pepper in a food processor until nuts are finely ground. Place pecan mixture in a large bowl. Add okra, tossing to coat. Gently press pecan mixture into okra. Pour oil to a depth of 2 inches into a Dutch oven or cast-iron skillet; heat to 350 degrees. Fry okra, in batches, for 5 to 6 minutes, until golden, turning once; place on paper towels. Serves 6 to 8.

Country-Time Green Beans

1 lb. green beans
¾ t. butter
¾ T. all-purpose flour
¾ t. sugar
⅓ c. chicken broth, warmed

¾ t. cider vinegar
pepper to taste
3 slices bacon, crisply cooked and crumbled

Boil green beans in water, uncovered, for 2 minutes. Drain; plunge beans into cold water. Drain; cut off stems and ends. Set aside. Melt butter in a skillet over medium heat; whisk in flour until smooth. Combine sugar and broth in a small bowl; add to flour mixture. Bring to a boil; stir for one minute. Reduce heat; mix in vinegar without boiling. Season with pepper; add beans and bacon. Heat through. Serves 6.

Sheri Fuchser
Goodlettsville, TN

"The secret to perfect green beans every time? Don't snap off the ends of fresh green beans until they've been cooked and cooled."

—Sheri

Crunchy Green Bean Salad

supper in a snap

Pair this crisp salad with pork chops and baked sweet potatoes. Microwavable sweet potatoes make the meal no-fuss.

½ c. honey
⅛ t. cayenne pepper
1½ c. pecan halves
3 T. sherry vinegar
2 t. Dijon mustard
¾ t. salt
½ c. walnut oil

2 lbs. green beans, trimmed
¾ c. sweetened dried cranberries
2 heads Belgian endive, trimmed and sliced lengthwise
pepper to taste

Combine honey and cayenne pepper in a saucepan over medium heat until warm. Stir in pecans; pour mixture onto a parchment paper-lined baking pan. Bake, uncovered, at 350 degrees for 8 minutes, or until golden, stirring occasionally. Remove from oven; set aside. Combine vinegar, mustard and salt. Slowly drizzle in oil, whisking to blend. Place green beans in a stockpot and cover with water; bring to a boil, reduce heat to medium and cook for 2 minutes, or until tender. Drain; plunge into ice water. Drain, pat dry and place in a serving bowl. Toss with vinegar mixture. Add nut mixture and remaining ingredients. Toss gently. Serves 12.

Fran Jimenez
Granite Bay, CA

Harvest Vegetables

Roasted and slightly garlicky in flavor, these vegetables are everyone's favorites!

2 lbs. **butternut squash**, halved, seeded and cut into 1½-inch cubes
2 lbs. **redskin potatoes**, quartered
2 to 3 **red onions**, quartered
16-oz. pkg. **baby carrots**
4 to 6 cloves **garlic**, pressed
3 T. **olive oil**, divided
2 t. **coarse salt**, divided
¼ t. **pepper**, divided
Optional: chopped **chives**

Combine vegetables and garlic; spread evenly onto 2 lightly greased baking sheets. Toss with oil, salt and pepper. Bake at 450 degrees for 40 to 50 minutes, tossing vegetables and rotating sheets from top to bottom of oven halfway through. Serve hot or at room temperature. Sprinkle with chives, if desired. Serves 8.

Jo Ann
Gooseberry Patch

Confetti Coleslaw

For an extra-special garnish, cut slits lengthwise in green onions and arrange on top of the coleslaw...mandarin orange sections placed at the tip of each green onion will resemble a flower.

3 c. **coleslaw mix**
¾ c. **frozen corn**, cooked and drained
¼ c. **red pepper**, diced
¼ c. **green pepper**, diced
4 T. **green onions**, chopped and divided
11-oz. can **mandarin oranges**, drained and divided
½ c. **mayonnaise**
2 T. **sugar**
1 T. **raspberry vinegar**
1 T. **lime** or **lemon juice**

Combine coleslaw mix, corn, red pepper, green pepper, 3 tablespoons green onions and oranges, reserving 6 orange sections for garnish. Mix together mayonnaise, sugar, vinegar and juice; blend well. Pour over salad and toss to coat well. Spoon into serving dish. Garnish with reserved orange sections. Serves 8.

Dale Evans
Frankfort, MI

Avocado + Fennel Salad

Check the ripeness of an avocado by gently pressing the stem end into the center of the avocado. There will be no resistance when it's ready to eat.

"My go-to recipe for a special salad."

–Jo Ann

2 avocados, halved, pitted and sliced
2 T. lemon juice, divided
1 bulb fennel, cored and very thinly sliced
½ red onion, thinly sliced
8 c. arugula leaves, torn
½ c. fresh cilantro
¼ c. olive oil
coarse salt and pepper to taste

Sprinkle avocado slices in a bowl with one tablespoon lemon juice. Toss gently to coat. Add remaining lemon juice, fennel and onion; set aside. Combine remaining ingredients in a large serving bowl; mix gently. Top with avocado mixture; toss gently. Serve immediately. Serves 4 to 6.

Jo Ann
Gooseberry Patch

Yoya's Spring Peas

Yoya is our family nickname for Grandma, who has passed this recipe along to the grandkids. These very tender, tasty peas have become a favorite with us.

1 c. butter, sliced
½ head iceberg lettuce, very thinly sliced
2 10-oz. pkgs. frozen petite peas
½ to 1 t. sugar

Melt butter in a large saucepan over medium heat. Add lettuce and sauté until soft. Add frozen peas and sugar; stir. Reduce heat to low. Simmer for about one hour, stirring occasionally. Serves 8.

Chris Larcel
Covina, CA

Anna Rae's Baby Limas

This is for folks who like a little spice in their lima beans!

1 c. water
1 cube chicken bouillon
16-oz. pkg. frozen baby lima
  beans
1 slice bacon, chopped

1 clove garlic, lightly pressed
⅛ to ¼ t. red pepper flakes
¼ c. butter, softened
salt and pepper to taste

Bring water and bouillon cube to a boil in a saucepan over medium heat; stir. Add beans, bacon, garlic and red pepper flakes. Cover and reduce heat to low. Cook for 25 minutes, or until beans are tender. Drain; stir in butter, salt and pepper. Serves 5 to 6.

Juanita Proffitt
Pickens, SC

"Anna Rae is my granddaughter who loves good ol' Southern cooking. She also loves any kind of vegetable, which is odd for a five-year-old!"

—Juanita

Sautéed Greens + Warm Pecan Dressing

A delectable way to serve greens fresh from the garden. Yum!

2 T. balsamic vinegar
1 T. mustard
2 t. honey
½ c. pecans, coarsely chopped

2 T. canola or olive oil
1 to 2 bunches kale, spinach
  or Swiss chard, chopped

Combine vinegar, mustard, honey and pecans in a small bowl; set aside. Heat oil in a large skillet over medium heat. Add greens and toss until well coated with oil. Cook and stir until greens are wilted but still bright green. Add vinegar mixture to skillet, stirring lightly. Cook for about one more minute and serve immediately. Serves 6.

Gloria Lopez
Austin, TX

supper in a snap

Ham is the perfect accompaniment to greens. Sauté ham steaks in a little butter and honey on each side until browned.

Cordie's Spicy Baked Beans

½ lb. ground pork sausage
½ green pepper, chopped
½ onion, chopped
2 15-oz. cans pork & beans, drained
½ c. catsup
⅓ c. brown sugar, packed
1 T. chili powder
1 t. mustard

Brown sausage with green pepper and onion in a large saucepan over medium heat; drain. Add remaining ingredients; mix well. Simmer for 15 minutes over medium heat, stirring frequently. Serves 4 to 6.

Pat Beach
Fisherville, KY

"My mother created this recipe more than 40 years ago...ever since, we have served these scrumptious baked beans at our family get-togethers."

—Pat

Warm German Potato Salad

10 lbs. redskin potatoes
1 lb. bacon, chopped
½ c. cider vinegar
1¼ c. water
1¼ c. onion, finely chopped
4 T. sugar
2½ t. salt
5 eggs, hard-boiled, peeled, sliced, and divided
sugar and salt to taste
Garnish: paprika

Cover potatoes with water in a large stockpot. Boil until soft but not falling apart; drain. Add bacon to stockpot and fry until crisp. Remove bacon, reserving 4 tablespoons drippings in stockpot. Add vinegar, 1¼ cups water, onion, sugar and salt. Cook for 5 to 7 minutes over medium heat, stirring occasionally; remove from heat. Meanwhile, peel and slice warm potatoes. Add potatoes to stockpot along with bacon and 4 sliced eggs; stir until well coated. Add sugar and salt to taste; spoon salad into a large serving bowl. Top with remaining sliced egg and sprinkle with paprika. Let stand before serving; serve warm. Serves 20.

Herbed Mashed Potatoes
Vickie (Gooseberry Patch)

6½ c. potatoes, peeled and cubed
2 cloves garlic, halved
½ c. milk
½ c. sour cream
1 T. butter, softened

2 T. fresh oregano, minced
1 T. fresh parsley, minced
1 T. fresh thyme, minced
¾ t. salt
⅛ t. pepper

Place potatoes and garlic in a large saucepan; cover with water. Bring to a boil over medium-high heat. Reduce heat to medium; simmer for 20 minutes, or until potatoes are very tender. Drain; return potatoes and garlic to pan. Add remaining ingredients; beat with an electric mixer at medium speed to desired consistency. Serves 6 to 8.

Spicy Baked Chili Fries

"My husband loves these French fries and always requests them. Serve them fresh and hot from the oven... make sure you have plenty of napkins!"

–Jo

1 t. chili powder
1 t. onion powder
1 t. garlic powder
1 t. seasoned salt
3 T. olive oil

3 baking potatoes, cut into wedges
Garnish: catsup or ranch salad dressing

Mix spices in a large container with a tight-fitting lid. Add oil and stir; add potato wedges. Place lid on container and seal tightly; shake vigorously to coat potatoes well. Arrange potatoes on an aluminum foil-lined baking sheet. Bake at 400 degrees for 15 minutes. Turn potatoes over and bake for 15 more minutes, or until tender and golden. Serve with Fry Sauce, catsup or ranch dressing for dipping. Serves 4 to 6.

Fry Sauce:

½ c. catsup

½ c. mayonnaise

Stir together catsup and mayonnaise in a bowl.

Jo Blair
Afton, WY

Spanish Rice

"When my three sons were little, they would want me to make this for our church potlucks...that way they knew there would be something there that they liked."

–Bobbi

1½ lbs. ground beef
2 10¾-oz. cans tomato soup
¼ c. green pepper, chopped

Optional: ¼ c. onion, chopped
1½ c. instant rice, cooked

Brown beef in a large skillet over medium heat; drain. Add tomato soup, green pepper and onion, if using; mix well. Add rice, stirring gently. Simmer for 15 minutes. Serves 8 to 10.

Bobbi Crosson
Toledo, OH

Grandmother's Garden Macaroni Salad

8-oz. pkg. elbow macaroni, cooked

2 c. cooked ham, diced

1 c. Cheddar cheese, cubed

15-oz. can peas, drained

1 tomato, diced

½ c. green pepper, diced

¼ c. onion, diced

1 t. salt

¼ t. pepper

¾ to 1 c. zesty Italian salad dressing

Combine all ingredients except salad dressing in a large bowl. Add dressing to taste. Toss and chill for one hour before serving. Serves 6 to 8.

Sandy Carpenter
Washington, WV

"My grandmother used to prepare this recipe when the whole family got together. We didn't live close by, so when we visited, everyone would drop in."

—Sandy

Mom's Macaroni + Cheese

supper in a snap

Make this kid-friendly favorite ahead and refrigerate before baking. While it bakes, slice warm store-bought rotisserie chicken and steam some green beans.

8-oz. pkg. elbow macaroni, uncooked
5-oz. can evaporated milk
1 c. milk
⅓ c. water
3 T. butter

3 T. all-purpose flour
1½ t. salt
1 T. dried, minced onion
1½ c. shredded sharp Cheddar cheese, divided

Cook macaroni according to package instructions; drain. Combine evaporated milk, milk and ⅓ cup water; set aside. Melt butter in a medium saucepan over medium heat. Add flour and salt, whisking until blended. Add onion and evaporated milk mixture, stirring well to avoid lumps. Add one cup cheese. Simmer until cheese melts and sauce thickens, stirring frequently. Stir in macaroni. Pour into a lightly greased 8"x8" baking pan. Top with remaining cheese and bake, uncovered, at 350 degrees for 30 minutes, or until bubbly and lightly golden. Serves 4 to 6.

Jenny Newman
Goodyear, AZ

Cheesy Polenta Bake

1 t. olive oil
1 green pepper, chopped
2 cloves garlic, minced
2 green onions, chopped
14-oz. jar marinara sauce
¼ c. shredded fontina cheese

¾ c. shredded mozzarella
  cheese
16-oz. tube polenta, cut into
  ¼-inch slices
½ c. grated Parmesan cheese

"This casserole is very rich...a small serving is just right!"
—Brenda

Heat oil in a saucepan over medium-high heat. Stir in green pepper, garlic and onions; cook for 3 minutes, or until pepper softens. Pour in marinara sauce; simmer for 5 to 7 minutes, stirring occasionally. Combine fontina and mozzarella cheeses in a small bowl. Spread a thin layer of sauce in a lightly greased 8"x8" baking pan. Arrange ⅓ of the polenta slices in the pan; top with ⅓ of the cheese mixture. Spoon a thin layer of sauce over cheese. Repeat layers twice. Top with Parmesan cheese. Bake, uncovered, at 350 degrees for 25 minutes, or until cheese is bubbly and golden. Serves 6 to 8.

Brenda Smith
Delaware, OH

Lemony Orzo Salad

16-oz. pkg. orzo pasta,
  uncooked
3 to 4 c. baby spinach
¼ c. olive oil
½ c. lemon juice
2 T. garlic powder
2 T. onion powder

2 t. fresh parsley, chopped, or
  1 t. dried parsley
1 t. salt
1 t. pepper
2¼-oz. can sliced black olives,
  drained
1 c. grape tomatoes

Cook pasta according to package directions until just tender; drain. Place spinach in a large bowl; add hot pasta and let stand for 2 to 3 minutes to wilt spinach. Combine remaining ingredients except olives and tomatoes. Mix well; add to pasta. Stir in olives and tomatoes. Serve either warm or chilled. Serves 8 to 10.

Doreen Freiman
Lake Hiawatha, NJ

Sweet Apple Tarts,
page 248

short + sweet desserts

Desserts don't need to be difficult or only for special occasions. These sweet treats come together quickly so you can satisfy a craving during the week. Finish your meal with Chocolate Icebox Cake (page 225), Minty Fudge Cookies (page 233), Angel Ice-Cream Cake (page 241) or Summertime Strawberry Pie (page 244). Whether made ahead or whipped together in minutes, these delicious desserts will put a smile on everyone's face.

Grandma's Banana Cupcakes

toss-ins for a twist

You can drizzle jarred caramel sauce over the tops to make these yummy cupcakes extra special.

½ c. butter, softened
1¾ c. sugar
2 eggs
2 c. all-purpose flour
1 t. baking powder
1 t. baking soda
¼ t. salt
1 c. buttermilk
2 bananas, mashed
1 t. vanilla extract
Garnish: 24 toasted pecan
    halves, sliced banana

Beat butter and sugar in a large bowl with an electric mixer at medium speed until light and fluffy. Add eggs, one at a time, beating after each addition. Combine flour, baking powder, baking soda and salt; add to batter alternately with buttermilk, beginning and ending with flour mixture. Beat at low speed after each addition until blended. Stir in bananas and vanilla. Fill paper-lined muffin cups ½ full. Bake at 350 degrees for 18 to 25 minutes, until a toothpick inserted in center comes out clean. Remove to wire racks to cool completely; frost with Cream Cheese Frosting. Store frosted cupcakes in an airtight container in refrigerator. Garnish each cupcake with a pecan half and banana slice just before serving. Makes 1½ to 2 dozen.

Cream Cheese Frosting:

8-oz. pkg. cream cheese, softened
½ c. butter, softened
1 t. vanilla extract
⅛ t. salt
16-oz. pkg. powdered sugar

In a large bowl, beat cream cheese, butter, vanilla and salt with an electric mixer at medium speed until creamy. Gradually add powdered sugar, beating until fluffy.

Kelly Marcum
Rock Falls, IL

Cake Mix Brownies
Kathy Grashoff (Fort Wayne, IN)

A decadent and inexpensive dessert.

18¼-oz. pkg. devil's food cake mix
1 egg, beaten
⅓ c. oil

⅓ c. water
Garnish: chocolate frosting,
chopped walnuts

Stir together cake mix, egg, oil and ⅓ cup water in a bowl to make a thick batter. Spread in a greased 13"x9" baking pan. Bake at 350 degrees for 20 to 25 minutes. Cool; spread frosting over squares and sprinkle with walnuts. Cut into squares. Makes one dozen.

Chocolate Icebox Cake

3.4-oz. pkg. cook & serve
  vanilla pudding
3.4-oz. pkg. cook & serve
  chocolate pudding

3 c. milk, divided
2 sleeves graham crackers
Garnish: whipped cream,
  chocolate sprinkles

Prepare pudding mixes separately according to package directions, using 1½ cups milk for each one; cool slightly. Line the bottom of an ungreased 13"x9" baking pan with whole crackers. Line sides of pan with halved crackers. Spoon vanilla pudding over crackers. Cover with another layer of whole crackers; spoon chocolate pudding over crackers. Crumble remaining crackers over top. Refrigerate until chilled. At serving time, dollop individual portions with whipped cream; garnish with sprinkles. Serves 8 to 10.

Joan Trefethen
Fairborn, OH

"Surprise...this cake is pudding! This easy dessert is a family favorite."

—Joan

Simple Crumb Cake

18¼-oz. pkg. yellow cake mix
⅔ c. milk
⅔ c. oil

4 eggs, beaten
Garnish: powdered sugar

Combine cake mix, milk, oil and eggs. Spread into a greased 13"x9" baking pan. Bake at 350 degrees for 15 minutes; cool. Top with Crumb Topping. Bake for 17 more minutes. Cool. Sift powdered sugar on top. Serves 12.

Crumb Topping:

3 c. all-purpose flour
½ c. powdered sugar
½ c. brown sugar, packed

2 T. cinnamon
½ c. butter, melted
1 T. vanilla extract

Mix together flour, sugars and cinnamon in a large bowl. Mix butter and vanilla in a small bowl; pour into flour mixture. Stir until crumbly.

Mary Anne Acquisto
Pocono Summit, PA

"This recipe was handed down through the family from my great-grandmother. It's scrumptious and simple to make."

—Mary Anne

Gooey Toffee Scotchies

18¼-oz. pkg. yellow cake mix
½ c. brown sugar, packed
½ c. butter, melted and slightly
  cooled
2 eggs, beaten
1 c. cashews, chopped
8-oz. pkg. toffee baking bits

Beat cake mix, brown sugar, butter and eggs in a bowl with an electric mixer at medium speed for one minute. Stir in cashews. Press mixture into a greased 15"x10" jelly-roll pan; sprinkle with toffee bits. Bake at 350 degrees for 15 to 20 minutes, until a toothpick inserted near center comes out clean. Cool in pan and cut into bars or triangles. To serve, drizzle with warm Toffee Sauce. Makes about 2½ dozen.

Toffee Sauce:

¾ c. plus 1 T. dark brown
  sugar, packed
2 T. dark corn syrup
6 T. butter
⅔ c. whipping cream

Bring sugar, syrup and butter to a boil in a saucepan over medium heat. Cook for 2 minutes. Carefully stir in cream and simmer for 2 more minutes, or until sauce thickens. Keep warm.

Rhonda Reeder
Ellicott City, MD

"I'm always looking for desserts with toffee in them. These delectable bars are my new favorites!"

—Rhonda

white chocolate drizzle

Give pastries a special touch with a drizzle of white chocolate! Place white chocolate chips into a small plastic zipping bag and microwave for one minute, or until chips melt. Snip off a tiny corner of the bag and squeeze to drizzle; then toss the empty bag.

Peanut Butter Bars
Angela Sims (Willow Springs, IL)

With rich butterscotch frosting, these are no ordinary peanut butter bars...wow!

1½ c. graham cracker crumbs
1 c. butter, melted
16-oz. pkg. powdered sugar

1 c. peanut butter
12-oz. pkg. butterscotch chips

Combine graham cracker crumbs, butter, powdered sugar and peanut butter in a large bowl; mix well. Press into a greased 13"x9" baking pan; set aside. Melt butterscotch chips in a double boiler; spread over crumb mixture. Refrigerate; cut into bars when cool. Makes 2 dozen.

Glorified Grahams

24 graham cracker squares
½ c. butter, melted
½ c. brown sugar, packed
1 c. chopped pecans

Arrange graham cracker squares in a single layer on an ungreased 15"x10" jelly-roll pan. Mix together butter and brown sugar in a bowl; spoon over graham crackers. Sprinkle with nuts. Bake at 350 degrees for about 12 minutes. Remove to a wire rack. Cool completely; break into squares. Makes 2 dozen.

Helen Young
Colorado Springs, CO

"My boys liked to take these cookies to school for classroom parties... they're easy to carry and yummy to eat."
—Helen

Caramel Crispy Rice Bars

I received this recipe from an old friend. She said that these were always a big hit whenever she made them for her daughter's birthday treats at school, and was she ever right! They always disappear quickly whenever I make them.

2 10-oz. pkgs. marshmallows, divided
¾ c. butter, divided
12 c. crispy rice cereal, divided
14-oz. pkg. caramels, unwrapped
14-oz. can sweetened condensed milk

Combine one package of marshmallows and half of butter in a large microwave-safe bowl. Microwave on high setting for 2 minutes. Stir until smooth; microwave for one more minute. Stir in 6 cups cereal; mix well. Press mixture firmly into a greased 13"x9" baking pan using a greased spatula. Combine caramels and condensed milk in a microwave-safe bowl; microwave on high setting until caramels melt. Stir until smooth; spoon over cereal layer. Use remaining marshmallows, butter and 6 cups cereal to prepare second batch of cereal mixture; press on top of caramel layer. Let stand for 5 minutes; cut into squares. Wrap each square individually with plastic wrap. Makes 1½ to 2 dozen.

Ann Aulwes
Russell, IA

toss-ins for a twist

Add a layer of melted chocolate for even more decadence. Follow the directions provided, but drizzle melted chocolate over the caramel layer.

Oatmeal-Carrot Cookies

"My daughter Andrea loves these moist cookies. They're one of her favorites!"

—Diana

¾ c. butter or margarine
¾ c. brown sugar, packed
½ c. sugar
1¾ c. all-purpose flour, divided
1 egg, beaten
1 t. baking powder
¼ t. baking soda
½ t. cinnamon
1 t. vanilla extract
2 c. quick-cooking oats, uncooked
1 c. carrots, peeled and shredded
Optional: ½ c. raisins

Blend butter or margarine until soft. Add sugars and ½ cup flour; mix well. Add egg, baking powder, baking soda, cinnamon and vanilla; beat well. Add remaining flour; mix well. Stir in oats, carrots and raisins, if using. Drop by rounded teaspoonfuls onto ungreased baking sheets. Bake at 375 degrees for 10 minutes. Makes 3 dozen.

Diana Carlile
Chatham, IL

Muddy Pies

When I was growing up with my three sisters and two brothers, Mom always took time to make these for us. After school we'd find them still cooling on the wax paper…sometimes I'd scoop them up with a spoon to eat while they were still warm. Yum! What a great memory.

toss-ins for a twist

Once the cookies cool, dip the ends in melted white candy coating…so pretty!

½ c. milk
3 T. baking cocoa
2 c. sugar
½ c. creamy peanut butter
½ c. butter
2 c. long-cooking oats, uncooked
1 t. vanilla extract

Place milk, baking cocoa and sugar in a saucepan over medium heat; bring to a boil. Boil for 3 minutes. Remove from heat; add peanut butter, butter, oats and vanilla. Mix well. Cool until stiff enough to drop by spoonfuls onto wax paper. Cool. Makes about 2 dozen.

Rhonda Millerman
Cameron, WI

White Chocolate Macaroons

Dottie McCraw (Oklahoma City, OK)

Ready-made cookie dough makes these super simple.

18-oz. tube refrigerated white chocolate chunk cookie dough, at room temperature

2¼ c. sweetened flaked coconut
2 t. vanilla extract
½ t. coconut extract

Combine all ingredients; mix well. Drop by rounded teaspoonfuls onto ungreased baking sheets; bake at 350 degrees for 10 to 12 minutes. Cool on baking sheets for 2 minutes; remove to wire rack to cool completely. Makes 2 dozen.

Snowballs

Snowballs

Covered in coconut flakes...there'll be no snowball fights with these!

1 c. semi-sweet chocolate chips
⅓ c. evaporated milk
1 c. powdered sugar
½ c. chopped walnuts
1¼ c. sweetened flaked coconut

Combine chocolate chips and milk in a double boiler; heat over hot water until chocolate melts. Stir to blend well. Remove from heat; stir in powdered sugar and nuts. Cool slightly. Form into one-inch balls; roll in coconut. Makes about 2 dozen.

Hope Davenport
Portland, TX

"Here in South Texas we have to make these around the holidays, because they are the only snowballs we're going to see."
—Hope

Minty Fudge Cookies

One day I put together some ingredients I happened to have on hand, and it made a wonderful cookie. Everyone loves them...me included!

18¼-oz. pkg. chocolate fudge cake mix
½ c. oil
2 eggs, beaten
10-oz. pkg. crème de menthe chocolate chips

Mix cake mix, oil and eggs in a bowl; stir in baking chips. Drop by rounded tablespoonfuls on ungreased baking sheets. Bake at 350 degrees for 10 minutes. Makes 3 dozen.

Jill Duvendack
Pioneer, OH

toss-ins for a twist

For something different, try strawberry or lemon cake mix with white chocolate chips.

Chocolate Chip Tea Cookies

These little cookies look so pretty yet are easy to make.

"When a friend asked me if I would bake cookies for a fundraiser, I didn't hesitate...I knew just what recipe to reach for!"

–Michelle

1 c. butter, softened
½ c. powdered sugar
1 t. vanilla extract

2 c. all-purpose flour
1½ c. mini semi-sweet
    chocolate chips, divided

Beat butter and powdered sugar with an electric mixer at high speed until fluffy. Add vanilla; mix well. Gradually beat in flour; use a spoon to stir in one cup chocolate chips. Form into one-inch balls; place 2 inches apart on ungreased baking sheets. Bake at 350 degrees for 10 to 12 minutes. Remove to wire rack to cool. Place remaining chocolate chips in a small plastic zipping bag. Seal bag; microwave on high for about 30 seconds, until chips melt. Snip off a small corner of bag; drizzle chocolate over cool cookies. Chill for 5 minutes, or until chocolate sets. Makes about 4 dozen.

Michelle Sheridan
Upper Arlington, OH

Soft Peanut Butter Cookies

Brenda Tranka (Amboy, IL)

If you're a peanut butter fan, these cookies won't last long. You'll enjoy every last crumb! Don't forget to serve them with a tall glass of cold milk.

1 c. sugar
1 c. creamy peanut butter

1 egg, slightly beaten
1 t. vanilla extract

Combine all ingredients; mix well. Form dough into one-inch balls and place on an ungreased baking sheet. Use a fork to press a crisscross pattern into the top of each cookie. Bake at 325 degrees for 10 minutes, or until golden. Cool before removing from baking sheet. Makes 2 dozen.

Sunny Lemon Blossoms

Who knew you could make cookies from cake mix!

> "These pop-in-your-mouth treats are addictive! I only make them when company's coming... so we aren't tempted to eat them all ourselves!"
>
> —Tina

18¼-oz. pkg. yellow cake mix
3.4-oz. pkg. instant lemon
   pudding mix

4 eggs, beaten
¾ c. oil
non-stick vegetable spray

Combine cake mix, pudding mix, eggs and oil in a large bowl. Spray mini muffin cups with non-stick vegetable spray; fill cups ½ full with batter. Bake at 350 degrees for 12 minutes. Cool in muffin cups on a wire rack for 10 minutes; remove from muffin cups and cool completely. Dip each cupcake into Lemon Glaze to coat; shake off excess. Place on a wire rack set over a baking sheet; refrigerate until set. Makes 4 dozen.

Lemon Glaze:

4 c. powdered sugar
⅓ c. lemon juice
3 T. lemon zest

3 T. oil
3 T. water

Combine all ingredients in a large bowl; stir until smooth.

Tina Dillon
Parma, OH

super shakers

Use a sugar shaker to save clean-up time in the kitchen. It's ideal for dusting powdered sugar onto cookies and desserts warm from the oven.

Ice-Cream Tacos

The next time you want tacos, make them the dessert kind! These sweet treats are stuffed with ice cream, drizzled with hot fudge and finished with a cherry on top.

8 frozen round waffles, thawed
1 qt. chocolate ice cream, softened
½ c. mini marshmallows
½ c. hot fudge sauce, warmed
8 maraschino cherries with stems

"The kids will love these...they're so much fun to eat!"
–Kathy

Warm waffles; do not toast. Gently fold each waffle in half; place in a 13"x9" baking dish, open-side up, keeping the rows tight to maintain taco shape. Combine ice cream and marshmallows in a large mixing bowl; spoon evenly into waffle shells. Cover and freeze until firm. Before serving, drizzle with warmed hot fudge sauce and top each with a cherry. Serves 8.

Kathy Unruh
Fresno, CA

Quick + Easy Hot Fudge Sauce

⅓ c. milk
⅓ c. baking cocoa

⅓ c. shortening
1 c. sugar

Mix together all ingredients in a heavy saucepan over medium heat. Bring to a boil, stirring with a wooden spoon. Boil for 30 seconds; remove from heat and serve. May be refrigerated and used later. Makes 1½ to 2 cups.

Linda Reynolds
Cut Bank, MT

> "Tried & true, this delicious recipe was passed down from my grandmother and mom. It's been a favorite for decades, and I've been known to multiply it 12 times to make banana splits for the cross-country team my husband coaches."
>
> —Linda

Caramel Sauce

This is delicious over ice cream, pound cake or warm pie.

1 c. brown sugar, packed
¼ c. butter

¼ c. whipping cream

Combine all ingredients in a small saucepan over medium heat. Bring to a boil, stirring constantly. Boil for one minute. Remove from heat; cool. Refrigerate for one hour. Makes about one cup.

Irene Robinson
Cincinnati, OH

Peanut Butter Ice-Cream Topping

1 c. sugar
½ c. water

½ c. creamy peanut butter

Combine sugar and ½ cup water in a small saucepan; heat until mixture boils. Boil and stir for one minute, making sure that sugar dissolves. Remove from heat; stir in peanut butter. Pour mixture into a blender; whip until creamy. Cool; refrigerate. Makes about 1½ cups.

Brenda Sinning
Lennox, SD

toss-ins for a twist

Spoon some of this sauce into a blender with vanilla ice cream to make yummy peanut butter milkshakes!

No-Fry Fried Ice-Cream

This quick & easy dessert features ice-cream balls rolled in a crunchy cereal topping…mimicking the familiar Mexican ice-cream dessert.

6 c. honey-coated corn flake cereal, crushed
2 T. sugar
3 T. butter or margarine, melted
5 T. corn syrup
1 t. cinnamon

1 gal. vanilla ice cream, softened
Garnish: caramel ice-cream topping, whipped topping, additional cinnamon

toss-ins for a twist

Try other types of cereal to roll the ice cream in for different taste treats.

Combine cereal, sugar, butter or margarine, corn syrup and cinnamon; set aside. Shape ice cream into 3-inch balls; roll in cereal mixture, pressing mixture lightly to coat balls. Place ice-cream balls in muffin cups; freeze until ready to serve. To serve, place each ice-cream ball in a serving dish; garnish as desired. Makes 8.

Renee Lewis
Basin, WY

Mince Ice-Cream Pie

A new taste for mincemeat pie lovers…this is cool and creamy!

1½ qts. French vanilla ice cream, softened
1½ c. mincemeat pie filling
½ c. plus 2 T. chopped walnuts or pecans, divided

9-inch graham cracker pie crust
Optional: frozen whipped topping, thawed

Combine ice cream, mincemeat and ½ cup chopped nuts in a large bowl; mix well. Spread evenly in graham cracker pie crust; freeze pie for 2 to 3 hours, until firm. Before serving, spoon whipped topping over pie, if desired. Garnish with remaining nuts. Serves 8.

Jacque Thompson
Clarkston, WA

Ice-Cream Delight

This is really easy to prepare and as the name says, is an absolute delight!

12 ice-cream sandwiches
6½-oz. can chocolate-flavored
   whipped topping

12-oz. pkg. malted milk balls,
   crushed

Arrange 4 ice-cream sandwiches side by side on a serving platter. Spread a layer of whipped topping over sandwiches. Sprinkle with ⅓ of crushed candy. Repeat layers, ending with crushed candy. Freeze for 3 hours. Serves 8 to 10.

Kristen Oudshoorn
Ridgely, MD

Angel Ice-Cream Cake

1 pt. whipping cream
3 T. sugar
1 t. vanilla extract
1 c. chopped pecans
18 coconut macaroons,
   crumbled

½ gal. rainbow sherbet,
   softened
½ gal. raspberry sherbet,
   softened
½ gal. vanilla ice cream,
   softened

Whip cream with sugar and vanilla until stiff peaks form; fold in pecans and cookie crumbs. Spoon half of mixture into a greased tube cake pan; layer rainbow and raspberry sherbet over top. Add a layer of vanilla ice cream; top with remaining whipped cream mixture. Cover; freeze overnight. Let stand for 5 to 10 minutes before serving; insert a knife around edge of pan to loosen. Cut into one-inch slices. Serves 12.

Kathleen Strunk
Mesa, AZ

"This recipe was served at a baby shower for my first daughter, Noelle. Due to a difficult pregnancy, her chance for survival was very slim. Thankfully, she did survive and 23 years later is a healthy, beautiful young woman. Each time I make this dessert, I am reminded that miracles do happen!"

–Kathleen

Ruby's Bavarian Cloud
Linda Kiffin (Tracy, CA)

3-oz. pkg. favorite flavored gelatin
mix
¼ c. sugar
1 c. boiling water
¾ c. chilled fruit juice or cold water
½ c. milk

½ t. vanilla extract
16-oz. container frozen whipped
topping, thawed
Garnish: crushed graham
crackers, chopped fruit,
whipped topping

Combine gelatin mix, sugar and 1 cup boiling water in a large bowl. Stir until gelatin dissolves. Blend in chilled fruit juice or cold water, milk and vanilla; blend in whipped topping. Top with crushed crackers, chopped fruit and whipped topping, if desired. Cover and refrigerate for 4 hours before serving. Serves 6.

Secret Ingredient Turtle Trifle

Believe me, your guests will have a hard time guessing that this quick & delicious dessert started with a frozen pecan pie!

32-oz. pkg. frozen pecan pie, thawed, cut into bite-size pieces and divided
8-oz. pkg. cream cheese, softened
8-oz. container frozen whipped topping, thawed
1 t. vanilla extract
⅓ c. fudge ice-cream topping
⅓ c. caramel ice-cream topping
½ c. chopped pecans

Layer half the pecan pie pieces in a large glass trifle bowl; set aside. Blend cream cheese, whipped topping and vanilla in a bowl until smooth. Spoon half of mixture over the pecan pie pieces; repeat layers. Drizzle with toppings; sprinkle with pecans. Refrigerate before serving. Serves 15 to 20.

Brenda Hager
Nancy, KY

toss-ins for a twist

Try chopped pumpkin pie or apple pie instead of pecan… just as yummy!

nuts about nuts

For a quick dessert garnish, toast nuts in a small dry skillet. Cook and stir over low heat for 3 to 4 minutes, until golden. Cool, place in plastic zipping bags and freeze. Ready to sprinkle on pies, cakes or ice cream whenever you want to add a little pizazz!

Summertime Strawberry Pie

1 qt. strawberries, hulled and
  divided
1 c. sugar
3 T. cornstarch
3-oz. pkg. cream cheese,
  softened
9-inch pie crust, baked
Optional: whipped cream

Reserve half of the biggest strawberries; set aside. Place remaining strawberries, about 1½ cups, in a blender. Process until smooth. Add water to puréed berries, if needed, to equal 2 cups; pour into a small saucepan. Add sugar and cornstarch; bring to a boil and cook for one minute, stirring. Remove from heat; cool. Spread cream cheese in bottom of pie crust; arrange reserved berries on top, pointed-end up. Pour cooled strawberry sauce over top. Cover and refrigerate for 2 hours. Top with whipped cream, if desired. Serves 8 to 10.

Christina Hubbell
Jackson, MI

Fresh Fruit Parfaits

"I made this dessert for a dinner party 20 years ago and got rave reviews. Parfaits without topping can be kept about 24 hours in the refrigerator, if nobody sneaks them before then!"

—Barbara

3.4-oz. pkg. favorite-flavor
  instant pudding mix
2 c. milk
2 c. assorted fruit, such as
  berries, cherries, grapes,
  peaches, pears, apricots,
  bananas or kiwi, cut up
  (no citrus or melon)
1 to 3 t. sugar or honey
Garnish: whipped cream

Combine pudding mix and milk; prepare pudding according to package directions. While pudding is setting, combine fruit in a bowl. Lightly toss with sugar or honey to taste. Layer fruit and pudding alternately in 4 parfait glasses. Garnish with whipped cream and serve immediately or cover and refrigerate for up to 24 hours and garnish at serving time. Serves 4.

Barbara Doebele
Olathe, KS

Summertime Strawberry Pie

Cherry Dream Pie

Perfect for picnics and potlucks.

8-oz. pkg. cream cheese, softened
½ c. powdered sugar
8-oz. container frozen whipped topping, thawed

9-inch graham cracker pie crust
14½-oz. can cherry pie filling

Blend cream cheese and powdered sugar together until smooth and creamy; fold in whipped topping. Spread into pie crust forming a well in the center; fill with pie filling. Refrigerate until firm before serving. Serves 6 to 8.

Clara Buckman
Waverly, KY

Banana Cream Pie

In the heat of summer, a chilled cream pie is a wonderful dessert. It's so simple to make…few things could be easier!

toss-ins for a twist

This is even better with fresh sliced bananas folded into the filling.

2¾ c. cold milk
2 3.4-oz. pkgs. instant vanilla pudding mix
2 T. banana extract
Optional: 5 drops yellow food coloring

8-oz. container frozen whipped topping
9-inch graham cracker crust

Whisk together milk, pudding mix, banana extract and food coloring, if using, for 3 minutes, or until softly set. Fold in whipped topping. Spoon into crust. Cover; freeze overnight. Thaw in refrigerator for one hour before serving. Serves 6 to 8.

Jennifer Niemi
Nova Scotia, Canada

Cherry Dream Pie

Berry Cream Tarts

"These cream-filled tarts look like you went to a lot of effort, but they're a snap to make. What a luscious way to serve dewy-fresh berries from the farmers' market!"

—Diana

10-oz. pkg. frozen puff pastry
  shells, thawed
¼ c. milk
¼ c. brown sugar, packed
8-oz. pkg. cream cheese,
  softened
½ c. sugar
½ t. cinnamon
1½ c. favorite berries
Optional: whipped topping

Place pastry shells on a lightly greased baking sheet. Brush shells with milk and sprinkle with brown sugar. Bake at 375 degrees for 10 to 15 minutes, until shells turn golden. Remove from oven and remove tops of shells; set aside. Blend together cream cheese, sugar and cinnamon in a bowl. Spoon 2 tablespoons of cream cheese mixture into each shell; top with berries. Replace tops. Return filled shells to oven and bake for 5 more minutes, or until filling is warm and bubbly. Top with whipped topping, if desired. Makes one dozen.

Diana Chaney
Olathe, KS

Sweet Apple Tarts

toss-ins for a twist

Try sliced peaches, nectarines or even pineapple in place of the apples.

1 sheet frozen puff pastry,
  thawed
½ c. apricot jam
3 to 4 Granny Smith apples,
  peeled, cored and sliced
⅓ c. brown sugar, packed
½ t. cinnamon
½ c. pistachio nuts, chopped
Optional: vanilla ice cream

Roll pastry into a 12-inch square on a lightly floured surface. Cut pastry into nine 3-inch squares. Arrange squares on an ungreased baking sheet; pierce with a fork. Spoon jam evenly over each square; arrange apple slices over jam. Combine brown sugar and cinnamon in a small bowl; mix well. Sprinkle over apple slices. Bake at 400 degrees for 20 to 25 minutes, until pastry is golden and apples are crisp-tender. Sprinkle with nuts. Serve warm topped with scoops of ice cream, if desired. Makes 9.

Jill Ball
Highland, UT

Brenda's Fruit Crisp

5 c. frozen peaches, apples or
  berries, thawed and juices
  reserved
2 to 4 T. sugar
½ c. long-cooking oats,
  uncooked
½ c. brown sugar, packed
¼ c. all-purpose flour

¼ t. nutmeg
¼ t. cinnamon
¼ t. vanilla extract
Optional: ¼ c. sweetened
  flaked coconut
¼ c. butter, diced
Optional: vanilla ice cream

Place fruit and juices in an ungreased 2-quart casserole dish; stir in sugar
and set aside. Mix oats, brown sugar, flour, nutmeg, cinnamon and vanilla
in a medium bowl. Stir in coconut, if using. Add butter to oat mixture;
combine until mixture is the texture of coarse crumbs. Sprinkle over fruit.
Bake at 375 degrees for 30 to 35 minutes, until topping is golden and fruit is
tender. Serve warm topped with ice cream, if desired. Serves 6.

Easy Cherry Cobbler

Melonie Klosterhoff (Fairbanks, AK)

15-oz. can tart red cherries
1 c. all-purpose flour
1¼ c. sugar, divided
1 c. milk
2 t. baking powder

⅛ t. salt
½ c. butter, melted
Optional: vanilla ice cream
   or whipped cream

Bring undrained cherries to a boil in a saucepan over medium heat; remove from heat. Mix flour, one cup sugar, milk, baking powder and salt in a medium bowl. Pour butter into 6 one-cup ramekins; pour flour mixture over butter. Add cherries; do not stir. Sprinkle remaining sugar over top. Bake at 400 degrees for 20 to 30 minutes. Serve warm with ice cream or whipped cream, if desired. Serves 4 to 6.

Blackberry Crumble

1⅓ c. all-purpose flour
½ t. baking soda
⅔ c. butter, softened
1 c. brown sugar, packed
1½ c. quick-cooking oats,
  uncooked

1 qt. blackberries
3 T. cornstarch
¾ c. sugar
⅛ t. salt
Optional: vanilla ice cream
  or whipped cream

Mix together flour, baking soda, butter, brown sugar, and oats with a fork until pea-size crumbles form; set aside. Combine blackberries, cornstarch, sugar and salt in a large heavy saucepan. Gently mash some berries, leaving about half of them whole. Bring to a boil over medium-high heat, stirring constantly. Reduce heat to medium; cook until mixture thickens. Pour into a lightly greased 13"x9" glass baking pan; crumble topping over berries. Bake at 350 degrees for 30 minutes, or until lightly golden. Serve with ice cream or whipped cream, if desired. Serves 8 to 10.

Marji Nordick
Meridian, ID

"My cousins and I used to pick blackberries in Grandma's backyard so she would bake us a crumble. The biggest, juiciest berries were always out of reach, so we had to climb on top of the old shed to get them. They were worth the work...and the scratches from thorns!"

—Marji

Sweet Apple Dumplings

2 Granny Smith apples, peeled,
  cored and quartered
cinnamon to taste
8-oz. tube refrigerated crescent
  rolls

½ c. butter, melted
1 c. orange juice
1 c. sugar
Optional: vanilla ice cream
  or whipped cream

Toss apple quarters with cinnamon; set aside. Separate crescent rolls; wrap each apple quarter in a roll. Arrange in a lightly greased 13"x9" baking pan. Combine butter, orange juice and sugar; blend well. Drizzle over wrapped apples. Bake at 350 degrees for 28 to 30 minutes, until golden and apples are tender. Serve warm with ice cream or whipped cream, if desired. Serves 8.

Becca Jones
Jackson, TN

"This recipe is a family favorite and has been used often for special occasions as well as weekday suppers. It is very easy to prepare. I hope you enjoy it as much as we do!"

—Becca

METRIC EQUIVALENTS

The recipes that appear in this cookbook use the standard U.S. method for measuring liquid and dry or solid ingredients (teaspoons, tablespoons, and cups). The information in the following charts is provided to help cooks outside the United States successfully use these recipes. All equivalents are approximate.

METRIC EQUIVALENTS FOR DIFFERENT TYPES OF INGREDIENTS

A standard cup measure of a dry or solid ingredient will vary in weight depending on the type of ingredient.
A standard cup of liquid is the same volume for any type of liquid. Use the following chart when converting standard cup measures to grams (weight) or milliliters (volume).

Standard Cup	Fine Powder (ex. flour)	Grain (ex. rice)	Granular (ex. sugar)	Liquid Solids (ex. butter)	Liquid (ex. milk)
1	140 g	150 g	190 g	200 g	240 ml
¾	105 g	113 g	143 g	150 g	180 ml
⅔	93 g	100 g	125 g	133 g	160 ml
½	70 g	75 g	95 g	100 g	120 ml
⅓	47 g	50 g	63 g	67 g	80 ml
¼	35 g	38 g	48 g	50 g	60 ml
⅛	18 g	19 g	24 g	25 g	30 ml

USEFUL EQUIVALENTS FOR LIQUID INGREDIENTS BY VOLUME

¼ tsp	=				1 ml
½ tsp	=				2 ml
1 tsp	=				5 ml
3 tsp	= 1 Tbsp		= ½ fl oz	=	15 ml
	2 Tbsp	= ⅛ c	= 1 fl oz	=	30 ml
	4 Tbsp	= ¼ c	= 2 fl oz	=	60 ml
	5⅓ Tbsp	= ⅓ c	= 3 fl oz	=	80 ml
	8 Tbsp	= ½ c	= 4 fl oz	=	120 ml
	10⅔ Tbsp	= ⅔ c	= 5 fl oz	=	160 ml
	12 Tbsp	= ¾ c	= 6 fl oz	=	180 ml
	16 Tbsp	= 1 c	= 8 fl oz	=	240 ml
	1 pt	= 2 c	= 16 fl oz	=	480 ml
	1 qt	= 4 c	= 32 fl oz	=	960 ml
			33 fl oz	=	1000 ml = 1 liter

USEFUL EQUIVALENTS FOR DRY INGREDIENTS BY WEIGHT

(To convert ounces to grams, multiply the number of ounces by 30.)

1 oz	=	¹⁄₁₆ lb	=	30 g
4 oz	=	¼ lb	=	120 g
8 oz	=	½ lb	=	240 g
12 oz	=	¾ lb	=	360 g
16 oz	=	1 lb	=	480 g

USEFUL EQUIVALENTS FOR LENGTH

(To convert inches to centimeters, multiply the number of inches by 2.5.)

1 in			=	2.5 cm	
6 in	= ½ ft		=	15 cm	
12 in	= 1 ft		=	30 cm	
36 in	= 3 ft	= 1 yd	=	90 cm	
40 in			=	100 cm	= 1 meter

USEFUL EQUIVALENTS FOR COOKING/OVEN TEMPERATURES

	Fahrenheit	Celsius	Gas Mark
Freeze Water	32° F	0° C	
Room Temperature	68° F	20° C	
Boil Water	212° F	100° C	
Bake	325° F	160° C	3
	350° F	180° C	4
	375° F	190° C	5
	400° F	200° C	6
	425° F	220° C	7
	450° F	230° C	8
Broil			Grill

index

main courses

Our Story

Back in 1984, we were next-door neighbors raising our families in the little town of Delaware, Ohio. Two moms with small children, we were looking for a way to do what we loved and stay home with the kids too. We had always shared a love of home cooking and making memories with family & friends and so, after many a conversation over the backyard fence, **Gooseberry Patch** was born.

We put together our first catalog at our kitchen tables, enlisting the help of our loved ones wherever we could. From that very first mailing, we found an immediate connection with many of our customers and it wasn't long before we began receiving letters, photos and recipes from these new friends. In 1992, we put together our very first cookbook, compiled from hundreds of these recipes and, the rest, as they say, is history.

Hard to believe it's been over 25 years since those kitchen-table days! From that original little Gooseberry Patch family, we've grown to include an amazing group of creative folks who love cooking, decorating and creating as much as we do. Today, we're best known for our homestyle, family-friendly cookbooks, now recognized as national bestsellers.

One thing's for sure, we couldn't have done it without our friends all across the country. Each year, we're honored to turn thousands of your recipes into our collectible cookbooks. Our hope is that each book captures the stories and heart of all of you who have shared with us. Whether you've been with us since the beginning or are just discovering us, welcome to the **Gooseberry Patch** family!

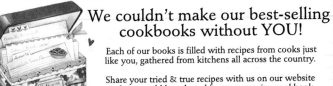

We couldn't make our best-selling cookbooks without YOU!

Each of our books is filled with recipes from cooks just like you, gathered from kitchens all across the country.

Share your tried & true recipes with us on our website and you could be selected for an upcoming cookbook. If your recipe is included, you'll receive a FREE copy of the cookbook when it's published!

www.gooseberrypatch.com

We'd love to add YOU to our Circle of Friends!

Get free recipes, crafts, giveaways and so much more when you join our email club...join us online at all the spots below for even more goodies!